RIDE GUIDE

New Jersey Mountain Biking

by Joshua M. Pierce

White Meadow Press

RIDE GUIDE New Jersey Mountain Biking
Copyright 1997 by Joshua M. Pierce

Cover: *photo by Joshua M. Pierce; design by Andrea Burke*

Maps: *Richard Widhu*

ISBN: 0-933855-13-3
Library of Congress Catalog Card Number: 97-61517

Also available:
Bed, Breakfast and Bike Mid-Atlantic
Bed, Breakfast and Bike New England
Bed, Breakfast and Bike Northern California
Bed, Breakfast and Bike Pacific Northwest
RIDE GUIDE North Jersey 2nd Edition
RIDE GUIDE Central Jersey
RIDE GUIDE Hudson Valley New Paltz to Staten Island 2nd Edition

Send for our catalog:
Anacus Press, Inc.
P.O. Box 4544
Warren, NJ 07059

Published by
WHITE MEADOW PRESS
a Division of

P.O. Box 4544, Warren, New Jersey 07059

ACKNOWLEDGMENTS

Special thanks to my parents, who taught me how to ride a bike without training wheels in Suburbia at the age of five.

To Greg, Scott, and Pat, who rode with me all around the state in the course of writing this book.

To the fruity kids of Route 18, who embodied the joy of mountain biking back when I rode poorly on my green, custom bent GT.

To summertime, without whose respite from the world of snow I would never have put away my skis and started riding a mountain bike in the first place.

To Fisher Price, the maker of Big Wheels and the Green Machine, who first introduced me to the wheel and the unbridled speed of self-propulsion.

CONTENTS

RIDING IN NEW JERSEY

Riding in New Jersey is a unique experience. It is characterized by a plethora of small local, county and state parks, each acting as an oasis from the hustle and bustle of the primarily urban nature of the state. I have ridden in enough other places to realize the differences between the vast expanses of the Colorado Rockies, the high deserts of Moab and Arizona, or the green mountains of New England, and the enclosure of New Jersey. Don't mistake me; some of the best riding I have ever done was here, but there is a difference.

When you start a ride on the Porcupine Rim Trail outside Moab, Utah, you get a sense of the vastness of the area and the danger surrounding the ride. Last year, two young men couldn't get out of a canyon after they took a wrong spur off the main trail. Their bodies weren't found for two months. That just doesn't happen around here unless automatic weapons and concrete leg anchors are involved. I do multiple laps at most of the places I ride. At Killington, Vermont, one loop riding up to the peak and back down again pretty much fills up the entire day. But there are places in New Jersey that I can go after work at 8 p.m., ride several loops with a headlight strapped to my helmet, then head out to a bar before closing time.

Of course, there are some relatively vast parks in New Jersey. Generally, the farther north and west you travel, the less civilized things become. At Allamuchy there are hundreds of miles of interconnecting trails to get lost on. The last time I went to Ringwood State Park, I ended up on the wrong side of a mountain and had to ride twenty miles on roads in New York State to get back to the car.

The terrain in New Jersey parks is extremely diverse. There is a ridge of small mountains running southwest to northeast across the state that separates two distinct types of terrain and topography. Southeast of that line are places like Hartshorne, Allaire, Clayton and Mercer, which lay in the relatively flat lands that make up most of the state. What they lack in hills and rocky terrain, they make up for with sand. Northwest of this line are wild, untamed places like Allamuchy, Ringwood and Mahlon Dickerson. There have been many times when I have been riding in these areas that I have stopped and said to myself that this can't really be New Jersey, the same state in which the turnpike is now sixteen lanes wide in spots. There are several areas along this ridgeline which take advantage of their location. Sourlands, White Rock and Lewis Morris are all great, hilly, technical places to ride very close to a huge population base. Two of the best places to ride in New Jersey, South Mountain and Watchung Reservation, are located along this ridge line. Both were closed to mountain biking in the spring of 1995 primarily due to the fact that they were overused and that there was so much tension between different trail user groups.

I have enjoyed countless moments of beauty on my bike, and I have found myself one with the world on countless singletrack trails all over the state of New Jersey. Please, go enjoy the splendor of our state on your bike, whether you are escaping the doldrums of your daily routine or celebrating life. Ride your old beat-up bike, replacing parts after every ride, or ride your rarely-used hybrid. Dust the cobwebs off your five-year-old garage fixture or break in your brand-new, tricked-out race machine with a higher resale value than your car. Ride slow, ride fast, respect the trail, respect the people you meet on the trail. Bring a friend and have fun.

DISCLAIMER

Mountain biking, like life, is an inherently dangerous activity. There are many factors that contribute to the difficulty of a trail. Many of these factors can and do change over time. Everything from erosion to storm damage, from weather conditions to direction of travel can alter the difficulty of any particular trail. At the present time, this book provides as accurate a description of these rides as possible. Many of the details will change over time.

This book is a guide. It is not a substitute for topographic maps, in-depth knowledge of a park, good judgment or common sense. If you feel you need more information on any particular park, call or write to their governing bodies; the addresses and phone numbers are included for every ride in this book. Or you can stop and talk to someone on the premises of most of the parks. They are there to help you.

It is your own responsibility to have an understanding of the routes you ride, the big rocks arbitrarily placed throughout a trail, the mechanical condition of your bike and your riding ability. Ride under control and within your own abilities, and always wear a helmet.

By purchasing this book or borrowing it from a friend, you have released Anacus Press, the author, and the artists from any liability for injuries you may sustain while using this book as a guide.

DEFINITIONS

BERMED TURN: Any turn in a trail in which the ground slopes down to the inside of the turn.

BRIDLE ROAD: see fire road.

DOUBLETRACK: Any trail giving more than one option of paths to take. Generally a Jeep trail that has two tracks worn away by automobile tires.

FIRE ROAD: Any primitive road constructed of dirt or gravel that is wide and open enough to provide a roadway for a serious four-wheel drive, off-road vehicle (see also doubletrack, bridle road).

LAND ACCESS/TRAIL ACCESS: Access to trails for bikes is a big issue virtually anywhere bikers, hikers and equestrians all enjoy the same trails. Land access has become a flashpoint in California and other places where highly concentrated populations of mountain bikers exist. With the closing of South Mountain Reservation and subsequently Watchung Reservation in the spring of 1995, it is evident that it has become a big issue in New Jersey as well. Many of the park rangers and parks commission officials I have talked to are not too enamored with the average mountain biker, and many have become increasingly angered by our presence in their parks in any capacity. There currently is an ordinance in Essex County making it illegal to ride a bicycle in any park in the county. In general, mountain biking is only allowed in a majority of the parks in the state by default. That is to say that mountain biking is allowed in most parks only because it has not been addressed specifically. Mountain bikers are guests in any park they visit.

LOOP: Any trail that reconnects with itself. A loop will start and finish at the same place.

OFF-CAMBER TURN: Any turn in a trail in which the ground slopes down to the outside of the turn. In general, an off-camber turn is tricky and requires a heightened sense of balance. The opposite of a bermed turn.

SINGLETRACK: Any trail for which there is only one possible and continuous line or track to take. Generally, single track has obstacles which it winds around, through and over, such as trees, rocks, logs, bushes or cliffs, which makes it necessary to navigate the single line

SPUR: A trail or portion of a trail which comes to a dead end or finishes without reconnecting with itself. If you ride a spur, you will have to take it in both directions or take a different trail to end up where you started.

SWITCHBACK: A turn in which the trail, traveling at an angle down a hill, turns back upon itself and begins traveling at a nearly 180-degree angle, but still down the same hill. It is an attempt in the construction of a trail to lessen the grade of the trail as it travels up or down a particular hill.

TECHNICAL: An adjective used to describe a type of trail that takes a lot of skill to negotiate. On opposite ends of the spectrum, riding on a flat, smooth, paved road is not very technical; riding up or down Mt. Rushmore would be about as technical as it gets.

TRAIL MAINTENANCE: Organized or unorganized means of protecting or rebuilding a trail in reaction to the destructive properties of bicycle tires, horse hooves or hiking boots. Everyone should participate in trail maintenance. If your favorite local riding spot becomes closed to biking and you haven't helped with any trail maintenance there, you really don't have any reason to complain.

TRIALS: A particular style of riding that involves locking both brakes and hopping from a standstill in order to navigate a particular obstacle. Observed Trials is a competitive category of racing wherein the rider must navigate a set of obstacles in whatever possible fashion without going out of bounds or touching the ground with his feet (dabbing).

WATERBAR: Usually a man-made structure designed to channel running water off a trail in the effort to minimize erosion. Waterbars are generally large, slippery pieces of wood running at an angle to the trail with a channel dug directly on the uphill side of them.

TRAIL RATINGS

All areas in this book are denoted by symbols explaining the range of difficulty at the top of the page in the Highlights Box. The symbols used in the box correspond to the range of rating of all the trails at the given area from easy to extremely difficult.

 EASY:

These are highly maintained trails containing only gradual grades and lacking any real obstacles. These trails are suitable for riders of any skill level. If you can ride a bike confidently down the road then this shouldn't be too much of a stretch for you.

■ **MODERATE:**

These trails contain moderate grades and are usually easy to get to and from. There are some obstacles or technical sections, generally interspersed with easier sections. If you can confidently clear a few logs that are lower than your front chainring then you should be all right. If you are not too confident in your riding abilities then you may spend some time walking your bike on these trails.

◆ **DIFFICULT:**

Difficult trails all contain something that sets them apart from the moderate ones. That tricky aspect could be constituted by loose rocky sections, boulder fields, numerous tall log obstacles, sketchy roots, long extended climbs or descents, or any combination of the above. Generally, a difficult trail is one where you can get seriously injured without trying too hard.

 EXTREMELY DIFFICULT:

These trails combine most or all of the elements included in a difficult trail, all at an accelerated pace. On one of these trails you can severely injure yourself even if you are trying to be safe. These trails can be frustrating or exhilarating, all depending on how your day is going.

ABUSIVE: Several of the routes in this book are rated as abusive in addition to extremely difficult. These routes, above being very difficult and requiring an expert level of skill to navigate, are physically and mentally draining and exhausting. These are not areas to be taken lightly. If it is only two or three hours until dark, don't begin riding Round Valley with the intention of finishing the entire fifteen-mile loop. If something goes wrong, you stand a very good chance of waiting overnight (or longer) before anyone comes by to save you.

This rating system is largely subjective and based on my own feelings towards the trails and areas as I have experienced them. There are many factors that go into the rating of any trail. Everything from speed to direction of travel on any given trail can change the feel or the difficulty of the ride. Conditions also change over time. A trail that I consider a moderate trail right now could become much more difficult or even dangerous over time due to erosion or lack of trail maintenance. Weather can also affect the difficulty of a trail. A lengthy drought can turn ordinarily enjoyable trails into tractionless sand pits, or certain trails can become mud pits for weeks after a good rain storm. Please, always practice common sense whenever you ride. Injuring yourself is never an enjoyable experience, and every accident brings mountain bikers closer to being locked out of our favorite areas.

The symbols for the general rating system were borrowed from the world of alpine skiing. They are intended to provide a uniform scale for all the areas in this book. This system is my own and does not directly correspond with any particular governing body's system. Some areas have not rated themselves at all for difficulty. Whenever a certain park uses its own rating system, I have included it. These ratings are explained in the trail classifications section of every individual area.

RIGHT OF WAY

Few, if any, trails in this state are set aside specifically for use by bikes alone. There are many trails set aside for foot traffic only, but not for bikes. As a result, all of the riding described in this book is on multi-use trails. All multi-use trails are subject to a right-of-way system. As a bicyclist it is easy to remember your responsibilities. Every other trail user takes precedence over bikers. You are obligated to yield the right of way to any hiker or equestrian you meet on any trail. Hikers have to yield to horses as well.

Also, there are some basic principles guiding responsibilities between bicyclists. If you come across another bicyclist in the woods, you should both slow down and get as far to the right side of the trail as possible to allow each other to pass. If you are going down a hill and there is not enough room to pass a rider you come across, it is your responsibility to slow down and yield the trail to the rider who is climbing the hill. If you are going down a hill you should be riding under control and in such a manner as to be capable of stopping or avoiding anyone you come across.

All trail users can get along and coexist, even in the congested parks of New Jersey. Horses, hikers and bikers are all capable of using the same trails. All that is needed is a little consideration. This past summer a friend and I were riding at Lewis Morris Park when we came upon two women on horseback who were a little lost. We helped them with their map and pointed out the way back to their parking lot. Since this was the way we were headed as well, they told us to try to keep up and galloped off. The next thing I knew I was riding hard up a beautiful singletrack in exhilarating pursuit of the horses.

MAP INFORMATION

The maps included in this book are current and up to date as of press time. Trails in parks are constantly being reconstructed and modified. They are not permanent. Changes in existing trails, closures of current trails and openings of new trails will occur over time. These maps are intended to be used only as an overall guide. You should check for any updates at the parks anytime you are exploring a new area or if you have not been to a specific park in awhile. An updated master map will generally be displayed on the premises. Also, more up to date trail maps will usually be available to take with you. If you cannot find trail maps, write or call the address or phone number listed with each individual park in this book.

The maps included in this book have come from various sources. Most have been compiled from existing trail maps in conjunction with other topographical maps, aerial maps, survey maps and tax maps. I have created a number of the maps specifically for this book where none existed.

All of the routes have been marked with arrows on the maps. The general format follows the following system:

→	First section of the route
⇨	Second section of the route when the route re-crosses or follows a previous section
⮑	Third section of the route when the route re-crosses or follows a previous section

The trail types follow this system:

●●●	Singletrack trail
■■■	Fire road, gravel road or doubletrack trail

The specific directions of the routes for each park are set up as follows:

Pt.-Pt.　　**Cume**　　**Turn**　　**Landmark**

Pt.-Pt. indicates the distance in miles from the last turn or point of interest. Point to point distances were calculated with an AVOCET 45 computer calibrated to an 80.24" wheel diameter for a WTB Velociraptor 26"x2.1" front tire. **Cume** is short for cumulative and is the total mileage from the starting point of the route. The abbreviations in the **Turn** column are:

L	Left
R	Right
S	Straight
BL	Bear Left
BR	Bear Right
SL	Sharp Left
SR	Sharp Right
X	Turn around

Additionally, a **T intersection** is one in which the trail you are on ends at the intersection and you must go either right or left to continue.

RIDE LOCATOR

1. **Hartshorne Woods Park—4.76 miles/4.91 miles**

2. **Huber Woods Park—5.48 miles**

3. **Clayton Park—6.5 miles**

4. **Manasquan Reservoir—5.16 miles**

5. **Allaire State Park—7.42 miles**

6. **Henry Hudson Trail—9.10 miles**

7. **Lewis Morris Park—5.29 miles**

8. **Mahlon Dickerson—7.67 miles**

9. **Sourlands Mountain Preserve—4.19 miles**

10. **Washington Valley Park—4.80 miles/8.41 miles**

11. **Delaware & Raritan Canal—28.02 miles/8.33 miles**

12. **Cheesequake State Park—3.60 miles**

13. **Round Valley Recreation Area—14.74 miles**

14. **Mercer County Park—13.04 miles**

15. **Ringwood State Park—6.57 miles/8.63 miles**

16. **Allamuchy State Park—7.90 miles**

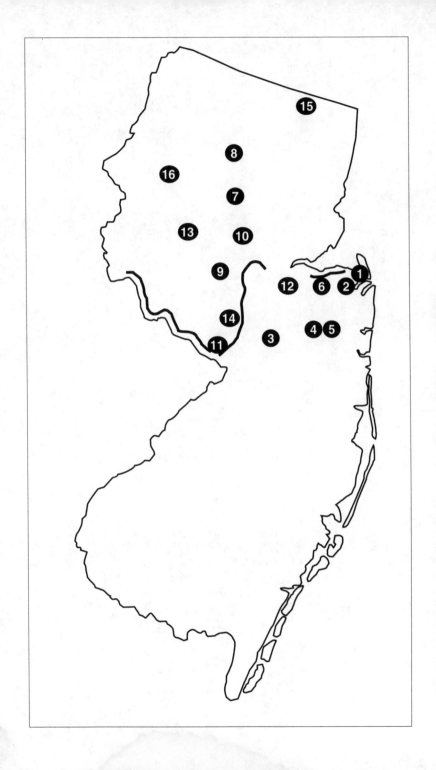

Hartshorne Woods Park—4.76/4.91 miles
Middletown, Monmouth Co.

HIGHLIGHTS ● - ◆

TERRAIN:	**Sandy, some roots, logs**
TOPOGRAPHY:	**Roller-coaster-esque, several longer climbs**
DIFFICULTY:	**Hybrid-friendly to difficult**
TRAIL TYPES:	**Mainly singletrack, some fire road**

GENERAL INFORMATION
Hartshorne Woods Park is a part of the Monmouth County Park System. For more information contact:

> Monmouth County Park System
> 805 Newman Springs Road
> Lincroft, NJ 07738-1695
> (732) 842-4000

DIRECTIONS: Hartshorne Woods Park is located off of Route 36 in the hills which make up the highest point on the Eastern seaboard of the U.S. The park is less than five miles from the Atlantic Ocean in Middletown, N.J. It can be reached by taking Exit 117 off the Garden State Parkway, or taking Route 35 to Route 36. Take Route 36 East twelve miles to the Scenic Dr. Exit. Turn right at the stop sign at the end of the off-ramp. The parking lot is less than half a mile on the left.

SIZE: Eleven miles of trails on 736 acres.

PARK HOURS: 8 a.m. to dusk, year round.

ENTRY FEE: No charge.

TRAIL CLASSIFICATIONS: All trails are marked by a symbol designating its accessibility and the skill level needed for completing the trail. All the trails in the Monmouth County Park System share this trail rating system:
Green Circles: indicate highly-maintained, gradual grade trails designed

primarily for walking.

Blue Squares: signify multiple-use trails with moderate grades and relatively easy access.

Black Diamonds: indicate steep grades, challenging terrain and minimal maintenance on trails designed for experienced bikers, hikers and equestrians.

TRAIL MAPS: There is a large trail map and information board in the Dismount Area by the parking lot. Trail maps are available there to take along.

RESTROOMS: There is a portable toilet by the Buttermilk Valley Trailhead and another one halfway around the Grand Tour Trail.

CLOSEST MOUNTAIN BIKING AREA: Huber Woods Park is only a few miles southwest in Locust, N.J. The eastern end of the Henry Hudson Trail is about three miles west of Hartshorne off Route 36.

OTHER PARK ACTIVITIES: Hiking, horseback riding and trail running are all popular activities at Hartshorne. All trails except the Candlestick Trail and the King's Hollow Trail, which are off-limits to bikes, are multi-use trails and are shared by all users.

OVERVIEW
Hartshorne is one of the most popular and heavily-trafficked mountain biking areas in New Jersey. With the closing of South Mountain Reservation and subsequently Watchung Reservation in 1995, even more mountain bikers have turned to Hartshorne for their source of off-road riding. As a result, it tends to get very crowded at Hartshorne on the weekends.

HISTORY: Hartshorne Woods Park's original owner was Richard Hartshorne, who first visited the area in 1670. Several years ago, the trails at Hartshorne were completely different than they are today. The trails were based around the Navesink Overlook (Candlestick Trail), which served as a hub for the multitude of trails that stemmed off it. In 1993, many of the existing trails that had become very rutted out due to overuse, were permanently closed off while the whole system of trails that exists today were cut and opened to public use. Soon, a number of the current trails will probably be closed and left to restore themselves to their natural status while new ones are opened.

DISMOUNT AREA: There is a strip of wide fire road about fifty yards long just off the Buttermilk Valley Trailhead and Parking Lot that is visibly posted from every direction with signs that read "Dismount Area." There is only one parking lot for Hartshorne Woods Park, and almost all the people using the area start and finish here. As a result, this is the most heavily congested area in the park. As a bicyclist, you are required to dismount and walk your bike through this section of trail. If courtesy and goodwill towards others aren't incentive enough for you to follow the rules, park rangers routinely wait at the bottom of the hill in this section and hand out tickets to anyone who tries to ride through the area.

CANDLESTICK TRAIL/KING'S HOLLOW TRAIL: These trails were made off-limits to bikes during the 1995 season and are designated as hiking trails only. Getting caught on your bike in this area will also result in a ticket.

TERRAIN/TRAIL COMPOSITION: Overall, the terrain at Hartshorne Woods is fast and dry in comparison to other New Jersey areas. The ground is very smooth, and there is a noticeable lack of exposed rock. The soil is somewhat on the sandy side, but given its location less than five miles from Sandy Hook, it is not nearly as sandy as you would expect. There are a few drawn-out hills at Hartshorne, but as a rule the hills are fairly short yet ferocious. The woods in this area are dense and surprisingly lush and deep green. Other than in the midst of a long dry spell or drought, the sandy surface reverts into a fine, smooth dirt, which mountain bike tires stick well to, but which is still very fast.

Within Hartshorne Woods there are any number of combinations of trails to ride. Hartshorne Woods Park itself uses a system for rating the difficulty of their trails that borrows the symbols from the world of alpine skiing. Candlestick and Kings Hollow Trails are designated easy walking trails and are demarcated by a circle. Laurel Ridge and Cuesta Ridge Trails are designated moderate and marked with a square. The Grand Tour Trail is designated challenging, for serious biking and hiking and is marked with a diamond. In reality though, these designations do not really apply once you get on a bike. The Candlestick Trail, when it was opened to mountain bikes, could be as challenging as any trail at Hartshorne, despite its designation as an easy trail. Everything from speed to direction of travel on any given trail can change the feel or even the difficulty of the ride. Though this is something that is generally true at most mountain biking areas, it is one of the very keys to riding at Hartshorne. While the Laurel Ridge Trail may have a gradual uphill culminating in a mad rushing downhill in the clockwise direction, climbing the same hill in the counter-clockwise direction is a much more difficult endeavor. Combining different sections of various trails with directional travel creates a seemingly endless number of different rides. My advice when riding Hartshorne is to explore as many trails as you can. Since the geographical size of the park is fairly small (736 acres), it is very hard to get lost for too long.

SPECIFIC TRAIL DIRECTIONS:
Beginner/Intermediate Ride: This route consists entirely of primitive, unpaved fire road and paved road. The overall structure is a 1.5-mile spur out to a 1.5-mile loop and back down the 1.5-mile spur to the parking lot. The spur climbs about 150 feet from the parking lot out to the paved loop, so it is a fun downhill at the end. The unpaved fire road portion of this route can be ridden without the paved section if you are looking for a shorter route. If at any point along the first mile and a half you feel as though you have gotten in over your head, turn around and head back down to the parking lot.

Total route distance: 4.76 miles
Ride time for a recreational rider: 1.0-1.5 hours

Pt.-Pt.	Cume	Turn	Landmark
			From the parking lot walk your bike into the **Dismount Area** and turn left onto the **Laurel Ridge Trail**. Walk your bike part way up the first incline before beginning to ride
0.00	0.00	**S**	Climb up the **Laurel Ridge** trail. This trail is a fire road. The hills are fairly steep and long. Don't fight, because there is plenty of loose gravel on the climbs for everyone
0.12	0.12	**S**	Up the loose gravel hill
0.08	0.20	**BL**	After the trail levels out it bears left and goes downhill for a short while
0.30	0.50	**S**	Start to climb up a long hill

Pt.-Pt.	Cume	Turn	Landmark
0.10	0.60	**S**	Top of hill. Go straight at the intersection. The fire road is relatively level with only small hills. At this intersection the **Laurel Ridge Trail** ends and the **Cuesta Ridge Trail** begins
0.77	1.37	**S**	Pass a right turn for the **Grand Tour Trail**
0.05	1.42	**BR**	Take the right fork to stay on the **Cuesta Ridge Trail**
0.13	1.55	**L**	Onto paved road (**Battery Loop**). If you feel you have gotten in over your head, you can turn around at any point and head back down to the parking lot.
0.10	1.65	**BL**	At five-way intersection. Pass one gate, cross another intersection and pass a second gate following signs for **Battery Loop**
0.41	2.06	**S**	At intersection. **Rocky Point** to the left goes to an overlook of the **Navesink River**
0.14	2.20	**S**	At intersection
0.05	2.25	**BL**	At the **steep grade** sign. Paved road goes down steep hill
0.05	2.30	**S**	Stay on **Battery Loop**. Left turn is for **Black fish Cove**, which will take you all the way down to a pier on the **Navesink River**
0.15	2.45	**S**	Start long, steep climb
0.37	2.82	**BL**	Pass Battery Lewis
0.15	2.97	**S**	Stay on paved road
0.06	3.03	**L**	Go past two gates and head back up **to Cuesta Ridge Trail**
0.12	3.15	**R**	Back onto **Cuesta Ridge Trail**. Follow it straight all the way back to parking lot
0.96	4.11	**S**	At intersection. Trail goes down *long, fast hill*
0.19	4.30	**S**	At bottom of hill
0.10	4.40	**BL**	Trail turns left and goes up one last short climb before going downhill back to parking lot
0.31	4.71	**S**	Get off bike at **Dismount Area**
0.02	4.73	**R**	In the heart of the **Dismount Area**
0.03	4.76		Back to parking lot. End of route

Advanced Loop: There are a number of popular advanced loops to be ridden at Hartshorne as the trails exist today. One of the most popular, and certainly one of my favorites, is described below. This loop is an advanced trail, and the majority of it is singletrack.

This route covers all the geographical regions of the park and approximately five of the eleven trail-miles, but it is by no means the only option in the park. My advice is to explore as many trails as you can. Several of my favorite sections of trail at Hartshorne aren't on this loop.

Total route distance: 4.91 miles
Ride time for an advanced rider: 0.5-1.0 hours

Pt.-Pt.	Cume	Turn	Landmark
			From the parking lot walk your bike into the **Dismount Area** and turn left onto the **Laurel Ridge Trail**. Walk your bike part way up the first incline before beginning to ride
0.00	0.00	S	Follow the fire road up, down and around. This series of hills is not very technical, but it usually seems to be the most painful part of this ride. I always feel like I'm riding in slow motion, no matter how hard I push
0.60	0.60	R	At the **top** of the second hill turn right onto the **Grand Tour Trail**. This trail is almost entirely **singletrack**. This is where the fun begins. After the first few turns, the trail widens out and dips downhill
0.27	0.87	L	Near the bottom of the steep, banked downhill take the left turn. This left fork levels out and becomes singletrack again. There are many log obstacles to cross in this section, and it is very roller-coaster-esque
0.70	1.57	S	Continue straight when a trail comes in from the left. This section contains a number of off-camber log crossings
0.21	1.78	R	Onto a wider, sandy trail
0.26	2.04	L	Stay on the **Grand Tour Trail**, which becomes singletrack again. **Do not** follow the **Trailhead** sign. You will pass a section of chopped-up tree trunks through one of the more mud-prone areas. Eventually you will pass a **cabin** on the

Pt.-Pt.	Cume	Turn	Landmark
			left (which may be obscured by foliage). Stay to the right
0.47	2.51	**R**	At the T where the singletrack dumps out onto a multitrack trail. You will pass another set of chopped-up trees and eventually come to a **short, but technical and grueling for the un initiated, climb**
0.43	2.94	**L**	There is an intersection at the top of the hill. The right trail is marked **"To Trailhead."** This is a quick way back to the parking lot if you have run out of daylight or feel that you have gotten in over your head. This is the halfway point for this loop. Turn **left** onto the **Laurel Ridge Trail.**
			There are no directional options for the rest of the loop. There are a few spurs off the trail, but the main trail takes you back to the Dismount Area
0.0	2.94		This first section is very fast. There is over half a mile of undulating hills which have an over all **downhill slant** to them. This is some of my favorite singletrack riding around. Enjoy!
0.53	3.47	**BR**	You will come to a log crossing followed by a right turn. From this point the longest uphill on the loop begins. It starts at a gradual grade and gets increasingly steeper
0.49	3.96		Shortly before the next downhill there is a left spur which leads out to the **Claypit Creek Overlook**, where there is a beautiful view of **the Navesink River**, especially in the fall or early spring when there are no leaves on the trees
0.00	3.96	**S**	The main trail continues and begins a very rug ged descent marred with switchbacks and nu merous waterbars
0.49	4.45	**S**	Eventually the trail levels out and continues to rise and fall over a number of smaller hills. Go straight at intersection
0.30	4.75	**S**	There is one last technical descent character-

Pt.-Pt.	Cume	Turn	Landmark
			ized by lots of loose rocks
0.13	4.88	**S**	The trail dumps you out right into the **Dismount Area**
0.03	4.91		Back to parking lot. End of route

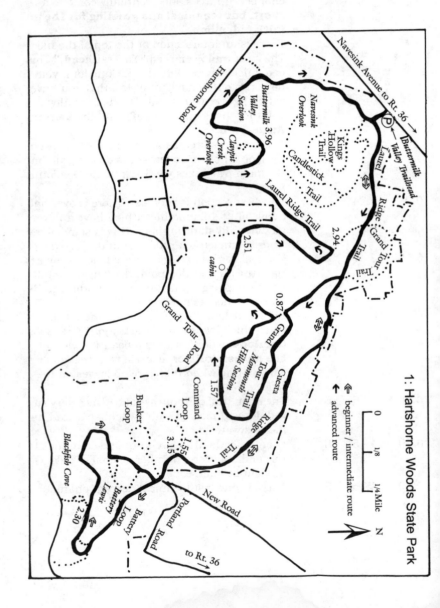

1: Hartshorne Woods State Park

Huber Woods Park—5.48 miles
Locust, Monmouth Co.

HIGHLIGHTS

TERRAIN:	Sandy, some roots, logs
TOPOGRAPHY:	Several long climbs, rolling hills
DIFFICULTY:	Moderate to difficult
TRAIL TYPES:	Mainly singletrack

GENERAL INFORMATION
Huber Woods Park is a part of the Monmouth County Park System. For more information contact:

> Monmouth County Park System
> 805 Newman Springs Road
> Lincroft, NJ 07738-1695
> (732) 842-4000

DIRECTIONS: Huber Woods Park is located in Locust, N.J., only a mile or so southwest of Hartshorne Woods Park. Take State Highway 35 to Navesink River Road. Take Navesink River Road 2.8 miles east to Brown's Dock Road. Turn left. The park entrance is at the top of the hill.

SIZE: Six miles of trails on 255 acres.

PARK HOURS: 8 a.m. to dusk, year round.

ENTRY FEE: No charge.

TRAIL CLASSIFICATIONS: All trails are marked by a symbol designating its accessibility and the skill level recommended for completion of the trail. All of the trails in all of the Monmouth County Park System share this trail rating system:
Green Circles: indicate highly-maintained gradual grade trails designed primarily for walking.
Blue Squares: signify multiple-use trails with moderate grades and relatively easy access.
Black Diamonds: indicate steep grades, challenging terrain and mini-

mal maintenance on trails designed for experienced bikers, hikers and equestrians.

TRAIL MAPS: Trail maps are available at the information center at the head of the trail at the parking lot.

RESTROOMS: There are public restrooms in the Environmental Center.

CLOSEST MOUNTAIN BIKING AREA: Hartshorne Woods Park is only a few miles northeast of Huber.

OTHER PARK ACTIVITIES: Walking, hiking, horseback riding.

OVERVIEW

Huber is very much like a younger sibling to Hartshorne in terms of mountain biking, although it is a substantial size on its own. Huber does not get as crowded with mountain bikes as Hartshorne, but on the other hand, there is not as much of a variety of terrain. As with Hartshorne, there are many different variations of interconnecting loops at Huber. My advice is to explore and come up with your own ride.

HISTORY: Huber Woods Park was established in 1974. The original Huber home, built in 1927, is now an environmental center. There is also an equestrian program center down the hill from the environmental center.

TERRAIN/TRAIL COMPOSITION: The terrain at Huber is very similar to that at Hartshorne. Overall the trails are fast and dry in comparison to other New Jersey areas. The ground is very smooth, and there is a noticeable lack of exposed rock. The woods in this area are dense and deep green. There are a plethora of fallen trees across the trails, more in certain areas than others. Most are ridable, depending on your ability level.

There are any number of combinations of trails to ride at Huber. Like all of the parks in the Monmouth County Park System, Huber uses a system for rating the difficulty of its trails which borrows its symbols from the world of alpine skiing. Circles demarcate easier trails. Moderate trails are squares and the most challenging ones are diamonds.

LINKING HUBER & HARTSHORNE ON BIKE: Hartshorne and Huber are less than two miles apart at their closest points, and linking the two parks by bike can amount to a day-long mountain bike adventure less than five miles from the Jersey Shore. From the trails at Huber, take Claypit Run out to Locust Point Road and turn left. Take the first right onto Locust Avenue and cross the bridge over the Navesink River. Turn right at the five-way intersection onto Navesink Avenue and take an immediate right onto Hartshorne Road. In less than half a mile there is a trailhead on the left side of the road. Take this trail up until it intersects with the Laurel Ridge Trail.

SPECIFIC TRAIL DIRECTIONS:
Intermediate/Advanced Loop: Huber Woods is a lot like Hartshorne. The hills are generally not as long as those at Hartshorne and there tend to be many more log obstacles. The biggest difference between the two parks is that Huber is very equestrian-friendly. There are horses all over Huber. There is an equestrian riding center at the park, and horses are allowed on every trail that mountain bikes are allowed to use. This loop is about five and a half miles long and uses about 85% of the trail-miles at Huber. Almost the entire route is singletrack.

Total route distance: 5.48 miles
Ride time for an intermediate rider: 1.0-1.5 hours

Pt.-Pt.	Cume	Turn	Landmark
0.00	0.00	**S**	From parking lot at information center, take thin trail straight across the field to the trailhead
0.06	0.06	**L**	Onto **Fox Hollow** trail. Winding singletrack
0.17	0.23	**L**	Turn **left** at fork onto **Meadow Ramble**
0.02	0.25	**S**	Across **Fire Road**. Stay on singletrack
0.03	0.28	**S**	Across maintained dirt road. Stay on singletrack. Trail starts to climb
0.16	0.44	**L**	Stay on **Meadow Ramble** trail
0.02	0.46	**R**	At first entrance to **Many Log Run**
0.53	0.99	**L**	At three-way intersection. Climb up loose, technical hill
0.05	1.04	**R**	At T intersection onto wider trail

Pt.-Pt.	Cume	Turn	Landmark
0.08	1.12	S	Come into meadow clearing. Head straight across to other side
0.04	1.16	S	Back into the woods on the other side of the clearing
0.07	1.23	R	Take the **right** fork
0.04	1.27	S	Take the middle of three branches. The trail becomes twisty singletrack with **lots** of log crossings
0.78	2.05	L	At fork onto the bottom half of the **Many Log Run**
0.54	2.59	L	Onto wider trail
0.02	2.61	BL	Stay on wider trail
0.04	2.65	BL	At clearing. Stay on the singletrack route on the edge of the meadow
0.11	2.76	S	Across maintained dirt road on a diagonal. Get back on singletrack on the other side
0.17	2.93	BR	At fork after large, built-up log pile
0.06	2.99	L	At the top of a *technical, rutted downhill with numerous waterbars*
0.26	3.25	L	At three-way intersection
0.01	3.26	L	Onto **Valley View**
0.38	3.64	R	At three-way intersection. Post sign says, "To Trailhead"
0.27	3.91	BL	Stay on trail as it bears left and another trail comes in from the right
0.25	4.16	S	Onto **Fox Hollow** at the trailhead intersection by the parking lot
0.16	4.32	S	At four-way intersection
0.02	4.34	R	At four-way intersection onto **Fox Hollow**
0.28	4.62	L	At three-way intersection onto singletrack
0.26	4.88	L	At top of technical climb
0.12	5.00	L	At top of *rutted downhill with several waterbars*
0.23	5.23	S	At four-way intersection. Stay on singletrack as it begins to climb
0.02	5.25	S	As trail comes in from the right. The trail gets steeper
0.17	5.42	R	At trailhead intersection. Ride up across field on singletrack

<u>Pt.-Pt.</u>	<u>Cume</u>	<u>Turn</u>	<u>Landmark</u>
0.06	5.48		Back to parking lot by Information Center. End of route

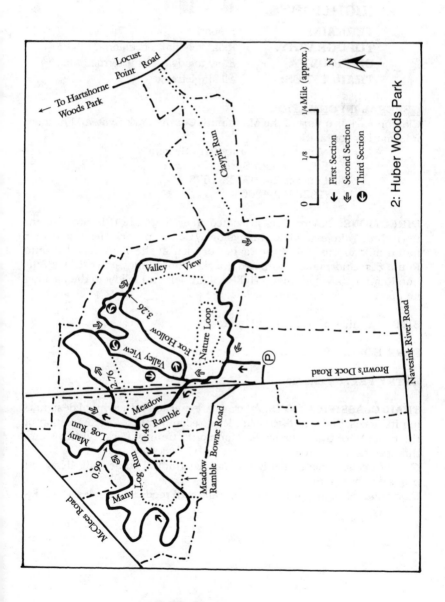

2: Huber Woods Park

Clayton Park—6.5 miles
Upper Freehold, Monmouth Co.

HIGHLIGHTS ● - ■

TERRAIN:	Smooth
TOPOGRAPHY:	Relatively flat, occasional hills
DIFFICULTY:	Easy to advanced intermediate
TRAIL TYPES:	All singletrack

GENERAL INFORMATION
Clayton Park is a part of the Monmouth County Park System. For more information contact:

> Monmouth County Park System
> 805 Newman Springs Road
> Lincroft, NJ 07738-1695
> (732) 842-4000

DIRECTIONS: Clayton Park is located off of Interstate 195 east of Allentown, N.J. Take exit 11 for Imlaystown/Cox's Corner. Head south for half a mile to the end of the road. Turn left at the T intersection onto Route 526 and make an immediate right onto Imlaystown-Davis Station Road. Follow to Emley's Hill Rd. Turn left and follow to the parking lot about 3/4 of a mile on the left.

SIZE: Six miles of trails on 391 acres.

PARK HOURS: 8 a.m. to dusk, year round.

ENTRY FEE: No charge.

TRAIL CLASSIFICATIONS: All trails are marked by a symbol designating its accessibility and the skill level recommended for completion of the trail. All of the trails in the Monmouth County Park System share this trail rating system:
Green Circles: indicate highly-maintained gradual grade trails designed primarily for walking.
Blue Squares: signify multiple-use trails with moderate grades and rela-

tively easy access.

Black Diamonds: indicate steep grades, challenging terrain and minimal maintenance on trails designed for experienced bikers, hikers and equestrians.

TRAIL MAPS: There is a large trail map and information board at the trailhead next to the parking lot.

RESTROOMS: There is a portable restroom by the information sign at the trailhead by the parking lot.

NEARBY MOUNTAIN BIKING AREAS: Clayton Park is very isolated from the rest of the Monmouth County parks. Mercer County Park near Princeton is probably the closest area.

OTHER PARK ACTIVITIES: Hiking, walking and horseback riding are all very popular at Clayton.

OVERVIEW
Clayton Park is one of the newest mountain biking areas in Central Jersey. It is largely undeveloped. It has been gaining popularity, however, due to its location less than ten miles from Exit 7A of the New Jersey Turnpike, and it does tend to get at least a few groups of riders at any time on the weekends.

TERRAIN/TRAIL COMPOSITION: Overall, the terrain is very fast at Clayton. The trails consist mainly of tight, winding singletrack. The terrain is relatively flat, with several extended hills. The ground is very smooth and there is a noticeable lack of rocks and roots.

SPECIFIC TRAIL DIRECTIONS:
Intermediate Loop: This route is a glorified figure eight. The entire route is 6.5 miles long. The main factor in the difficulty of this route is speed. Clayton is fairly speed friendly, but the route is going to be a lot more difficult at 10-15 mph than at 5 mph. If you are not a very strong rider or you want a shorter route, cut off either the first or second half and slow down the pace.

Total route distance: 6.50 miles
Ride time for an intermediate rider: 1.0-1.5 hours

Pt.-Pt.	Cume	Turn	Landmark
0.00	0.00		From the parking lot ride straight to the trailhead along the treeline next to the information board
0.02	0.02	S	Onto singletrack trail with several log pile obstacles to navigate
0.07	0.09	L	Onto wider multitrack trail
0.03	0.12	BR	Take the first branch to the right. After a stretch of level terrain, the singletrack dips downhill, and after a bit of fast, smooth descent, *starts to twist and turn tightly*
0.35	0.47	S	Cross the wooden footbridge at the bottom of the valley
0.05	0.52	R	At the T after the bridge
0.26	0.78	S	The trail will eventually come to a large **log pile**. There is a trail that circumnavigates the fallen tree if it looks too intimidating
0.04	0.82	R	Onto **Doctors Creek Trail.** Rutted-out down hill
0.08	0.90	S	Cross a bridge
0.03	0.93	S	Go straight across a wider trail. Stay on singletrack
0.26	1.19	L	At three-way intersection. Eventually come to fast, mild downhill
0.64	1.83	L	After the trail loops around, you will come to a four-way intersection. **Turn left**
0.51	2.34	S	Trail starts to climb a long, extended hill
0.48	2.82	R	At the very top of the hill. Trail is relatively flat for a short time. Watch out for a sharp right turn in the trail
0.03	2.85	BL	Very fast downhill begins. Beware of people climbing up the trail in the other direction
0.32	3.17	BL	Bear left, re-cross the bridge and climb the short, steep, granny gear hill back up to level ground
0.13	3.30	R	Onto the **Bridges Trail**
0.02	3.32	BR	Relatively flat. There are several fallen logs to navigate
0.49	3.81	R	Trail leads to a wooden footbridge. At the other end of the bridge you must go right.

Pt.-Pt.	Cume	Turn	Landmark
			There are several well-constructed water channels
0.21	4.02	**L**	Sign says **"Trailhead."** Start to climb straight up the wide trail
0.04	4.06	**BR**	Take the first singletrack offshoot to the right
0.25	4.31	**R**	Turn **right** back onto the wide trail
0.04	4.35	**R**	Onto singletrack just before coming out of the woods
0.11	4.46	**BR**	Back to parking lot. When you come out of the woods bear right. A dirt doubletrack road begins at the right end of the parking lot

SECOND HALF OF ROUTE:

Pt.-Pt.	Cume	Turn	Landmark
0.18	4.64	**R**	Stay on the dirt road. Follow it around the trees
0.14	4.78	**R**	Get onto the singletrack that hugs the treeline when the dirt road starts to lead away from the trees
0.06	4.84	**S**	Enter the woods. *Technical, fast and tricky downhill.* Can be dangerous. Singletrack downhill
0.16	5.00	**S**	Come out of the woods. Follow thin path around the pond
0.21	5.21	**BL**	Up a sandy, short hill to the left
0.05	5.26	**L**	Onto wider trail. Short sandpit section
0.02	5.28	**S**	Stay on **Bridges Trail.** Pass a right turn, which would take you back up to the parking lot
0.18	5.46	**L**	Pass a few waterbars and turn **left**
0.04	5.50	**SR**	After the bridge
0.02	5.52	**L**	Pass the right turn
0.12	5.64	**R**	Onto the **Bridges Trail**
0.02	5.66	**S**	Pass the left turn for **Doctors Creek Trail.** Cross the big log pile in the opposite direction from the beginning of the ride
0.31	5.97	**L**	After a hard right turn in the trail. Cross the bridge. Long, technical, leg-burning granny gear climb back towards the car

Pt.-Pt.	Cume	Turn	Landmark
0.39	6.36	**BL**	Get back onto the original multitrack trail
0.04	6.40	**R**	Onto the singletrack just before coming out into the clearing
0.07	6.47		Come out into the clearing by the information board
0.03	6.50		Return to parking lot; end of route

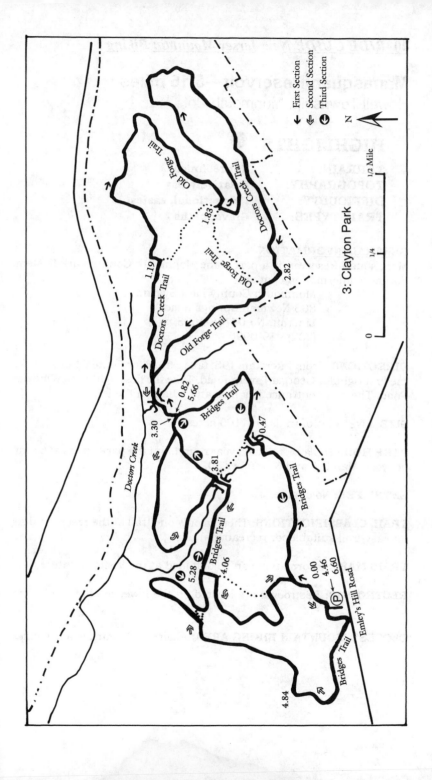

3: Clayton Park

First Section
Second Section
Third Section

N

1/2 Mile
1/4
0

Old Forge Trail

Doctors Creek Trail

Old Forge Trail

1.83

1.19

2.82

Doctors Creek Trail

Old Forge Trail

Doctors Creek

0.82
5.66

3.30

Bridges Trail

0.47

3.81

Bridges Trail

Bridges Trail

Bridges Trail

5.28

4.06

0.00
4.46
6.60

P

4.84

Bridges Trail

Emley's Hill Road

Manasquan Reservoir—5.16 miles
Howell Township, Monmouth Co.

HIGHLIGHTS

TERRAIN:	**Not technical**
TOPOGRAPHY:	**Relatively flat**
DIFFICULTY:	**Recreational, easiest**
TRAIL TYPES:	**Gravel paths**

GENERAL INFORMATION
Manasquan Reservoir is a part of the Monmouth County Park System. For more information contact:

> Monmouth County Park System
> 805 Newman Springs Road
> Lincroft, NJ 07738-1695
> (732) 919-0996

DIRECTIONS: From Interstate 195, take exit 28 for Route 9 North. Take the first right for Georgia Tavern Road. Take the first right onto Windeler Road. The main entrance is a mile and a half on the left

SIZE: Five miles of trails on 1100 acres.

PARK HOURS: 8 a.m. to dusk, year round, but the park opens at 6 a.m. between March 1 and November 30.

ENTRY FEE: No charge.

TRAIL CLASSIFICATIONS: There is only one trail at the reservoir. It is an easy trail suitable for recreational riding.

TRAIL MAPS: Information can be obtained at the Visitor Center.

RESTROOMS: Restrooms are located on the lower level of the Visitor Center.

CLOSEST MOUNTAIN BIKING AREA: Allaire State Park is a few miles east of Manasquan.

OTHER PARK ACTIVITIES: Walking, hiking, and horseback riding are permitted on the perimeter trail. Boating and fishing are both popular on the reservoir. Winter activities include ice skating, ice fishing and cross-country skiing.

OVERVIEW
There is only one trail at Manasquan. It is a perimeter trail that encircles the reservoir. This multi-access trail is open to hikers, horseback riders, bicyclists and pedestrians. During the summer it is a popular spot for all the above activities. The trail can accurately be described as recreational and non-technical.

HISTORY: Manasquan Reservoir was constructed in 1987. The reservoir has been serving utility companies and municipalities since 1990.

TERRAIN/TRAIL COMPOSITION: The trail is a gravel path that is connected by one roadway bridge and a series of footbridges.

SPECIFIC TRAIL DIRECTIONS:
Beginner/Recreational Loop: The trail at Manasquan is a perimeter trail that circumnavigates the reservoir. It is a recreational trail that is suitable for mountain bikes and hybrids. It is also a popular spot for walking and hiking.

Total route distance: 5.16 miles
Ride time for a recreational rider: 0.5-1.0 hours

Pt.-Pt.	Cume	Turn	Landmark
			From the parking lots at the main entrance, ride back towards the entrance
0.00	0.00	**L**	Follow sign for trail entrance and turn **left**. The route will travel in a **counter-clockwise** direction around the reservoir
0.05	0.05	**S**	Across paved entrance road. Pass gate
0.07	0.12	**S**	Pass the five-mile wooden marker on the left
0.21	0.33	**S**	Pass a **wooden gate**

Pt.-Pt.	Cume	Turn	Landmark
0.06	0.39	S	Across paved road
0.04	0.43	S	Pass a wooden gate. The trail goes downhill
0.55	0.98		Top of a long downhill grade
0.14	1.12	S	Pass the four-mile marker
0.10	1.22	S	Across a gravel road. Trail runs right next to a road
0.09	1.31	S	Cross a long, arched wooden footbridge
0.02	1.33	S	Across a gravel road
0.47	1.80	S	Across paved road
0.32	2.12	S	Pass the three-mile marker
0.16	2.28	S	Gravel path goes alongside reservoir. Cross boulder dike
0.44	2.72	S	Across dirt road
0.41	3.13	S	Pass the two-mile marker. The trail comes out and follows paved road across long bridge
0.34	3.47	S	Pass **Chestnut Point** parking lot
0.23	3.70	L	Trail turns left and heads away from road. It follows a gravel road for awhile
0.10	3.80	S	Pass a wooden fence
0.20	4.00	S	Enter a wooded area. The trail traverses a narrow finger of land bordered by water on both sides
0.13	4.13	S	Pass the one-mile wooden marker
0.07	4.20	S	Come out into clearing. Cross wooden foot bridge and re-enter woods
0.13	4.33	S	Cross wooden footbridge over stream
0.03	4.36	S	Cross wooden footbridge
0.56	4.92	S	Across gravel road. The trail becomes much wider
0.18	5.10	S	Pass a left turn to the parking lots
0.05	5.15	L	At original start point at wooden gate

4: Manasquan Reservoir

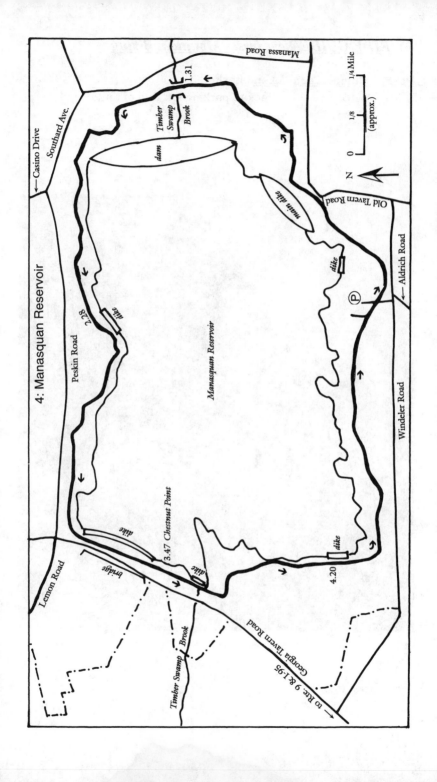

<u>**Pt.-Pt.**</u>	<u>**Cume**</u>	<u>**Turn**</u>	<u>**Landmark**</u>
0.01	5.16		Back to parking lot. End of route

Allaire State Park—7.42 miles
Farmingdale, Monmouth Co.

HIGHLIGHTS

TERRAIN:	Very sandy, some roots, logs
TOPOGRAPHY:	Many short hills, several longer ones
DIFFICULTY:	Easy to moderately difficult
TRAIL TYPES:	Mainly singletrack, some wider trails and fire roads

GENERAL INFORMATION
Allaire State Park is a part of the New Jersey State Park Service. For more information contact:

> Allaire State Park
> P.O. Box 220
> Farmingdale, NJ 07727
> (732) 938-2371

DIRECTIONS: These directions are not for the main entrance to Allaire State Park. They are for the multi-use trail parking lot on Hospital Road. There is no mountain biking from the main entrance, and if you do wind up there, you will be directed by a park ranger to the Hospital Road parking lot.

From Route 34 South, take the first right after the Parkway entrance at the first light. This is Allenwood Road. At the T intersection, turn right onto Atlantic Ave. Turn left at the first intersection onto Hospital Road. The parking lot is half a mile on the right.

Or, from Interstate 195, use exit 31A toward Lakewood. Take a left onto Herbertsville Road at the first intersection. Bear left onto Allenwood Road. Turn left onto Hospital Road. The parking lot is half a mile on the left.

SIZE: About nine miles of trails on a total of 3008 acres.

PARK HOURS: Trails open dawn to dusk, year round.

ENTRY FEE: There is no fee to use the multi-use trail located off of the Hospital Road parking lot. If you do enter the main gate to visit the historic Allaire Village, the entrance fee is $2.00 on weekdays and $3.00 on weekends and holidays from Memorial Day through Labor Day.

TRAIL CLASSIFICATIONS: There is only one marked trail at Allaire. It does not have any designated difficulty for mountain biking. I would consider it to be a moderate trail overall.

TRAIL MAPS: Trail maps are available at the gate at the main entrance to the park.

RESTROOMS: There are no facilities by the multi-use trail area.

CLOSEST MOUNTAIN BIKING AREA: Manasquan Reservoir is less than five miles west of Allaire in Howell. Hartshorne and Huber Woods are about 15 miles north.

OTHER PARK ACTIVITIES: Hiking, horseback riding, canoeing, fishing, hunting, camping and sightseeing.

OVERVIEW
Allaire State Park is predominantly an historical site around which camping, hiking and biking facilities have grown through numerous acquisitions of land under the Green Acres Program.

HISTORY: Allaire began as an iron forgery in the early 1790s. In 1822, the property was purchased by James P. Allaire, who turned the site into a self-contained community of up to 500 people. There he produced castings and pig iron for building steamship engines and boilers. The village declined in the 1840s, but the village was preserved by Arthur Brisbane, who purchased the property in 1907. In 1941, the property was deeded to the State of New Jersey and has tripled in size over the last fifty years.

TERRAIN/TRAIL COMPOSITION: The terrain at Allaire consists of rolling hills and sandy soil. Depending upon the weather and how much rainfall has recently accumulated, the soil can be extremely sandy and difficult to ride. In places it can be like attempting to ride on the beach at the ocean. If the weather has not been too arid, the trail should be fairly hardpacked except in a few spots. The sandy soil tends to become rutted out easily where large volumes of people have used the singletrack trail, especially on the steeper sections. There are numerous small log obstacles, but relatively few large obstacles at all on the trail. There is a noticeable lack of rocks at Allaire in general.

SPECIFIC TRAIL DIRECTIONS:
Intermediate Loop: There is only one mountain biking trail at Allaire, and it is well marked with small orange circles labeled with white arrows nailed to trees at every intersection. The markers are only facing in one direction. It is very difficult to try to follow the trail backwards. There are a plethora of interconnecting trails and dead-end spurs criss-crossing the marked trail. Once you become familiar with this trail, you can use these extraneous trails to link up your favorite sections of the marked trail, or to create new or multiple loop combinations within the multi-use trail area. The printed map is not very detailed except to say that the marked trail follows an overall counter-clockwise direction, but the actual trail is marked well enough that you should be able to follow it without getting lost. There are over forty intersections detailed in the route below. At times, it could get very confusing and frustrating trying to follow the written directions at every intersection. In these situations, it is probably easier to just follow the posted arrows unless you get to an intersection, which is poorly marked.

The only keys to getting back to the Hospital Road parking lot are that the loop is almost exactly seven miles long, and that when you get to a poorly paved, overgrown section of road, you are right by the short spur back to the parking lot.

Total route distance: 7.42 miles
Ride time for an intermediate rider: 1.0-2.0 hours

Pt.-Pt.	Cume	Turn	Landmark
0.00	0.00	S	From the west end of the **Hospital Road** parking lot, there is an information board with a trailhead next to it
0.04	0.04	R	Onto **fire road**, then immediately bear left onto **singletrack**. Trail runs parallel to the fire road
0.27	0.31	S	Across old, overgrown paved road

Pt.-Pt.	Cume	Turn	Landmark
0.02	0.33	**S**	Through intersection
0.37	0.70	**S**	Through intersection
0.14	0.84	**BL**	**Steep technical climb** beginning directly after left turn
0.16	1.00	**S**	Through intersection. **Deep sandy area**. Short hill climb
0.24	1.24		Another hill climb
0.06	1.30	**SR**	Follow orange arrow signs. Stay on singletrack. Trail becomes roller-coaster-esque
0.16	1.46	**BL**	Follow orange arrow signs to detour around extremely rutted-out section of trail
0.05	1.51	**S**	At three-way intersection. The trail eventually goes down a long hill
0.11	1.62	**S**	Through intersection at bottom of hill. Stay on singletrack
0.25	1.87	**S**	Through intersection at bottom of hill. Climb up another hill
0.21	2.08	**BL**	Onto thin singletrack
0.02	2.10	**BL**	Follow orange arrow signs
0.08	2.18	**S**	At three-way intersection
0.06	2.24	**BR**	Then **bear left** at clearing. Follow signs. Continue straight on main trail
0.08	2.32	**S**	Across intersection. Stay on wider trail
0.09	2.41	**R**	Onto singletrack. Short technical climb
0.15	2.56		Top of long singletrack downhill
0.01	2.57	**SL**	Twisty, technical singletrack trail
0.13	2.70	**BL**	Just before sandy fire road. Follow orange arrow signs off to the left on singletrack running parallel to fire road
0.39	3.09	**S**	Across very sandy fire road. Stay on singletrack
0.07	3.16	**BL**	Trail widens, **becomes extremely sandy** fire road. Beginning of a **long, basically unridable climb**. Follow fire road straight up the hill to the top
0.11	3.27	**L**	At top of hill. **Stay along treeline**. There is a wide-open clearing straight ahead with power line towers
0.09	3.36	**S**	Onto singletrack into the woods at the far end of the clearing. Follow large (2-foot-wide) orange

PtPt.	Cume	Turn	Landmark
			arrow sign
0.04	3.40	**S**	Through intersection
0.06	3.46	**S**	At three-way intersection. This section is relatively flat atop a mesa
0.06	3.52		Short, technical climb
0.24	3.76	**BR**	At intersection. Follow orange arrow signs. Trail widens out for awhile, then narrows back to singletrack
0.15	3.91	**R**	At three-way intersection
0.07	3.98	**S**	At three-way intersection
0.19	4.17	**S**	At intersection
0.17	4.34	**S**	At intersection
0.06	4.40	**S**	At three-way intersection
0.07	4.47	**SL**	At intersection
0.13	4.60	**S**	At intersection. There is a nearby street off to the right
0.25	4.85	**S**	At intersection. Pass a small green shack
0.17	5.02	**SL**	At five-way intersection
0.29	5.31	**L**	At three-way intersection
0.10	5.41	**R**	At three-way intersection
0.02	5.43	**R**	At three-way intersection onto wider trail
0.05	5.48	**R**	At four-way intersection. Stay on wider trail
0.13	5.61	**S**	At three-way intersection. Stay on wider trail
0.14	5.75	**SL**	At five-way intersection
0.24	5.99	**SR**	At three-way intersection onto singletrack trail
0.14	6.13	**L**	At four-way intersection onto wider trail
0.17	6.30		Follow arrows at the top of the hill
0.03	6.33	**L**	Onto fire road and stay to the left
0.24	6.57	**BL**	Onto singletrack. Continue **fairly straight** through multiple intersections. Follow the arrow signs
0.02	6.59	**BR**	At three-way intersection
0.03	6.62	**BR**	Onto roller-coaster-esque singletrack
0.16	6.78	**S**	At clearing. Follow the arrow signs. Stay up on the ridge
0.17	6.95	**L**	Onto overrun paved road. At this point ***do not*** follow arrow signs. They will send you back out onto the beginning of the loop again. **Continue past** the first set of arrow signs. Stay on the

Pt.-Pt.	Cume	Turn	Landmark
			paved/gravel road
0.15	7.10	**R**	Onto singletrack. The trail runs parallel to the paved/gravel road
0.25	7.35	**BL**	Come back out onto gravel road and cross to the left side
0.02	7.37	**BL**	Onto singletrack just before the gate by **Hospital Road**
0.05	7.42		Back to parking lot. End of route

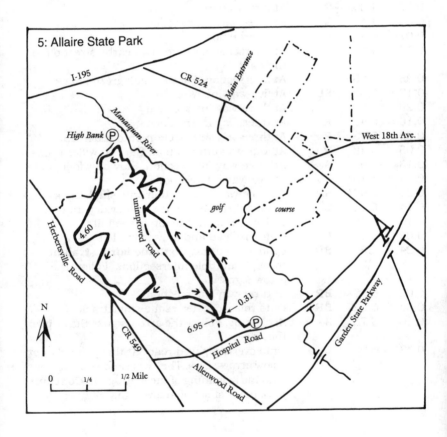

5: Allaire State Park

Henry Hudson Trail—9.10 miles
Aberdeen to Belford, Monmouth Co.

HIGHLIGHTS ●

TERRAIN:	**Smooth paved surface**
TOPOGRAPHY:	**Flat grade railbed**
DIFFICULTY:	**Recreational, non-technical**
TRAIL TYPES:	**Multitrack**

GENERAL INFORMATION

The Henry Hudson Trail is a part of the Monmouth County Park System. For more information contact:

> Monmouth County Park System
> 805 Newman Springs Road
> Lincroft, NJ 07738-1695
> (732) 842-4000

DIRECTIONS: The Henry Hudson Trail runs parallel to Route 36 from Aberdeen to Leonardo. There are three off-street parking areas which access the trail. One is at the intersection of Gerard Avenue and Lloyd Road in Aberdeen. Another is at the Memorial School and Scholer Park in Union Beach. The third is at McMahon Park in North Middletown. The route described below begins and ends at the western end of the trail in Aberdeen. These are directions to the Fireman's field parking lot.

From North: Take the Garden State Parkway south to exit 117A. After passing through the toll booth, turn left at the T intersection. The parking lot is just beyond the next traffic light on the left-hand side.

SIZE: Nine miles of trail.

PARK HOURS: Dawn to dusk, year round.

ENTRY FEE: No charge.

TRAIL CLASSIFICATIONS: There is only one trail. It is designated as

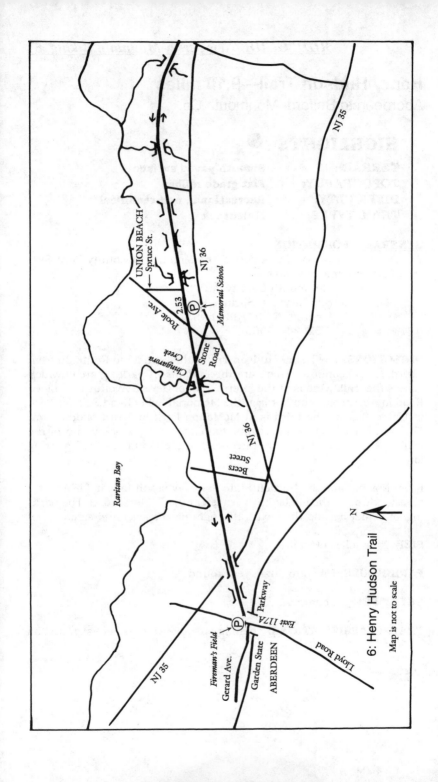

6: Henry Hudson Trail

Map is not to scale

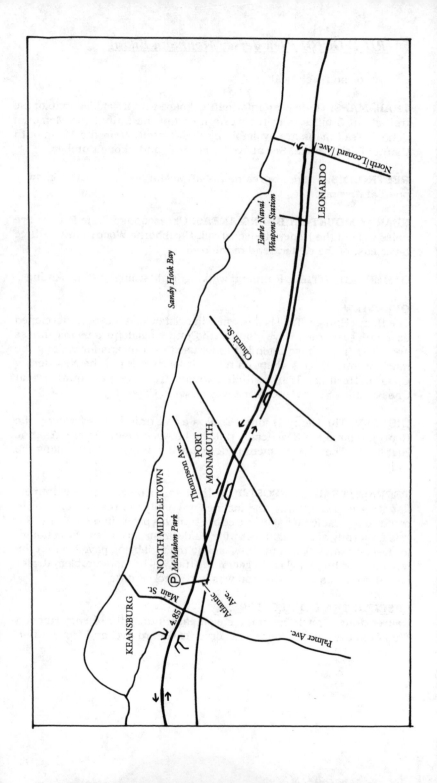

easiest, or non-technical.

TRAIL MAPS: There is an information board with a detailed map of the trail about 3 miles from the western end of the trail at the Memorial School. Trail maps are available by mail directly from the Monmouth County Park System. See above for address and phone number.

RESTROOMS: There are restrooms at McMahon Park at the midway point of the trail.

NEARBY MOUNTAIN BIKING AREAS: Cheesequake State Park is five miles west of the Henry Hudson Trail. Hartshorne Woods Park is three miles east of the eastern end of the trail.

OTHER ACTIVITIES: Running, walking, sightseeing, in-line skating.

OVERVIEW
The Henry Hudson Trail is fairly new in existence. It has been developed as a multi-use trail to give Monmouth County residents a usable fitness area. The trail is also intended to be used as a means for visiting the many historical sites along its route. It forms a leg of the New Jersey Coastal Heritage Trail, which extends from its headquarters at Cheesequake State Park all the way down to Cape May.

HISTORY: The Henry Hudson Trail is a rail-trail. It was formerly the Central Railroad of New Jersey rail line between Aberdeen and Atlantic Highlands. There are numerous designated points of interest along the trail.

TERRAIN/TRAIL COMPOSITION: The Henry Hudson trail is extremely flat. As a former railway, the inclines are limited to that which a train could comfortably manage. The entire trail was paved in the fall of 1996. It is uniformly about eight feet wide, and the surface is smooth enough for in-line skates. The only drawback to the trail being paved is that the tendency for broken glass to get on the trail will be more problematic for flats than it was when the trail was hard-packed dirt.

SPECIFIC TRAIL DIRECTIONS:
Recreational Spur: This route encompasses the entire Henry Hudson Trail from the parking lot on the corner of Gerard Ave. and Lloyd Rd. in

Aberdeen to the end of the paved trail at North Leonard Avenue in Belford.

The trail is a spur, which is nine miles long. The directions will only be travelling one way. Follow the directions backwards to get back to the start from the eastern end of the trail.

The route is pretty easily broken up into smaller sections. If you are looking for a shorter ride than the entire 18 miles, you can either start at the beginning of the route and turn around when you start to get tired, or you can start at one of the other two parking areas in the middle of the trail.

Total route distance: 9.10 miles (one way)
Ride time for a recreational rider: 2.0-3.0 hours (round trip)

Pt.-Pt.	Cume	Turn	Landmark
			Starting from the **Fireman's Field** parking lot at the corner of **Gerard Ave**. and **Lloyd Rd**. in **Aberdeen**, the trailhead is across the street, next to the Shell gas station
0.00	0.00	S	Enter onto the trail. **The entire trail is paved**
0.30	0.30	S	Cross a wooden bridge over the **Luppatatong Creek**
0.07	0.37	S	Cross bridge over **Route 35**
0.27	0.64	S	Cross **Beers Street**
0.19	0.83	S	Across a street. Pass the Marie Catrell playground
0.08	0.91	S	Across a street. Trail eventually comes out and runs parallel to a street
0.15	1.06	S	At stop sign by the Cornucopia Restaurant. Cross to the left side of the street
0.03	1.09	L	Re-enter the trail
0.17	1.26	S	Across a street
0.16	1.42	S	Across a street
0.18	1.60	S	Across a wooden bridge over the **Chingorora Creek**
0.12	1.72	S	Across **Stone Road**
0.27	1.99	S	Across **Florence**
0.23	2.22	S	Across **Poole Ave**. Trail runs parallel to a small street for awhile. Pass a school

Pt.-Pt.	Cume	Turn	Landmark
0.31	2.53		**Memorial School**. There is a large **information board** alongside the trail. There is a large, detailed map of the Henry Hudson Trail
0.06	2.59	S	Across **Spruce St.**
0.11	2.70	S	Across wooden bridge over **Flat Creek**
0.21	2.91	S	Across **Union Ave**. Pass the Union Beach Memorial Library, Goodies Ice Cream Parlor and Stevie G's sports bar. The trail runs parallel to Jersey Avenue for awhile
0.22	3.13	S	Across wooden bridge over creek. To the left there is a great view of the **Manhattan skyline** and the **Varazzano Narrows Bridge**
0.17	3.30	S	Across small wooden bridge over a small creek
0.14	3.44	S	Across street
0.10	3.54	S	Across arched wooden bridge over creek
0.30	3.84	S	Across small wooden bridge over wide creek
0.12	3.96	S	Across **Central Avenue**. The trail runs parallel to 6th Street for awhile
0.21	4.17	S	Across street
0.32	4.49	S	Across long wooden bridge over wide creek
0.07	4.56	S	Across **Creek Street**
0.06	4.62	S	Across **Church Street**
0.23	4.85	S	Across **Main Street** in **Keansburg**. Pass **McMahon Park** on the left. There are basketball courts, softball fields, ice skating rinks, a playground and restrooms at the park
0.61	5.46	S	Across **Atlantic Avenue**. Pass several softball fields on the left
0.16	5.62	S	Across **Thompson Avenue**. The trail runs right next to **Route 36** for the rest of the spur
0.27	5.89	S	Pass through gate in the thick concrete wall
0.08	5.97	S	Across small wooden bridge
0.34	6.31	S	Across road on a diagonal
0.14	6.45	S	Across **New Street** and **Main Street** in **Port Monmouth**. Pass the Middletown Train Caboose and train station on the left
0.13	6.58	S	Across street
0.40	6.98	S	Across wooden bridge over wide creek
0.11	7.09	S	Across **Church Street**

Pt.-Pt.	Cume	Turn	Landmark
0.19	7.28	**S**	Across a street
0.19	7.47	**S**	Across **East Road**
0.89	8.36	**S**	Cross entrance road for **Earle Naval Weapons Station**. Cross under a bridge
0.09	8.45	**S**	Cross **Broadway** at traffic light on Route 36
0.24	8.69	**S**	Cross **Appleton Avenue** next to the traffic light on Route 36
0.32	9.01	**S**	Cross **Thompson Avenue** next to the traffic light on Route 36
0.09	9.10	**X**	North **Leonard Avenue**. End of spur. To get back to Aberdeen, follow the directions in reverse

Lewis Morris County Park—5.29 miles
Morristown, Morris Co.

HIGHLIGHTS ■ - ■■

TERRAIN:	**Rooty in spots, relatively smooth overall**
TOPOGRAPHY:	**Big hills, steep and relatively long**
DIFFICULTY:	**Moderate**
TRAIL TYPES:	**Mainly singletrack, some fire road**

GENERAL INFORMATION
Lewis Morris is a part of the Morris County Park System. For more information contact:

> Morris County Parks Commission
> P.O. Box 1295
> Morristown, New Jersey 07962-1295
> (973) 326-7600

DIRECTIONS: From Interstate 287 take exit 35. Get onto South Street westbound and follow signs for Route 24 West through Morristown. The park entrance is about 3.5 miles on the left. Take the road up to the top of the hill and follow signs for Sunrise Lake.

SIZE: Eight miles of trails on 1,154 acres.

PARK HOURS: Dawn to dusk, year round.

ENTRY FEE: No charge.

TRAIL CLASSIFICATIONS: The Morris County Parks Commission does not offer a classification system of its own. I would consider all of the trails at Lewis Morris to be moderate to difficult. The biggest factor in rating the difficulty of the trails is the length and steepness of the hills. From an elevation of 350 feet at the main entrance and parking lot at Sunrise Lake, you have to climb to above 600 feet within the first half mile of riding. Once you get up top, there are a number of different loops that stay on top of the ridge.

TRAIL MAPS: There are trail maps at the parking lots at Sunrise Lake, Mendham Overlook Area, Sugarloaf Area and the Old Army Area. Individual trail maps can be obtained by writing to the Park Commission at the above address.

RESTROOMS: There are restrooms in the bath/boathouse at Sunrise Lake, as well as at the Sugarloaf, Doe Meadow and Old Army Area.

OTHER NEARBY MOUNTAIN BIKING AREAS: Allamuchy State Park and Mahlon Dickerson County Park are both within 25 miles of Lewis Morris.

OTHER PARK ACTIVITIES: Hiking, horseback riding, picnicking, swimming, softball, fishing, boating, and cross-country skiing.

OVERVIEW
Lewis Morris is a Morris County Park and is controlled by the Morris County Park Commission. The park is located just a few miles west of Morristown, making it the most popular riding spot in the area.

HISTORY: The park is named after New Jersey's first Governor, Lewis Morris, who was elected in 1738. It opened in March 1958 as a general purpose park.

TERRAIN/TRAIL COMPOSITION: Lewis Morris is situated in a very hilly region of the state. The main starting point for mountain biking, Sunrise Lake, is low in a valley at the northern end of the park. From here, all of the trails (except the Patriot's Path) climb up to the top of the ridge 250 vertical feet above. The terrain at Lewis Morris is somewhat of an anomaly. There is an incredible lack of exposed rock given the hilly nature of the park. There is a substantial amount of exposed roots, but the trails tend to be relatively smooth compared to any of the areas to the northwest.

The trails consist almost entirely of singletrack, and they tend to wind and meander every which way. The main structure of trails is based around gravel "bridle" roads, but even where the roads seem to be the most direct route between two points, there always seems to be a singletrack trail mirroring the road.

SPECIFIC TRAIL DIRECTIONS:
Intermediate/Advanced Loop: This route encompasses most of the trails in the park and all of the park's regions. Virtually the entire route is singletrack, except for the beginning and ending spur to and from the parking lot.

Total route distance: 5.29 miles
Ride time for an intermediate rider: 1.5-2.0 hours

Pt.-Pt.	Cume	Turn	Landmark
0.00	0.00	S	From the **information board** near the top of the parking lot at **Sunrise Lake**, head uphill
0.02	0.02	S	Onto narrow paved road that heads downhill
0.09	0.11	R	At bottom of hill onto gravel road
0.15	0.26	S	Enter the wooded area and continue **straight** on the gravel road as it passes a singletrack trail which comes down onto the road from the left
0.04	0.30	L	At three-way intersection. Get onto the **yellow blaze** trail, which heads straight up steep hill
0.03	0.33	L	Take the **left** fork. The trail becomes narrower and more technical
0.11	0.44	R	At three-way intersection. Continue on the **yellow blaze** trail. The trail takes a milder approach to the hill
0.11	0.55	R	Take the **right** fork. Stay on the **yellow blaze** trail. After a hard left turn, the trail begins to climb again
0.52	1.07	R	At three-way intersection. The trail is marked with **yellow and blue blazes**
0.11	1.18	S	The trail tops out and heads down a steep gravel hill. *Watch your speed*
0.10	1.28	SR	Directly at the bottom of the hill just before coming out to a bridle road. Stay on the **yellow blaze** trail. It becomes singletrack and crosses numerous log piles
0.37	1.65	S	Enter a swampy area at bottom of hill
0.02	1.67	S	Cross a stream. Trail starts a **long, grinding, technical climb**
0.17	1.84	R	At T intersection at top of hill onto level ground.

PtPt.	Cume	Turn	Landmark
			This section is marked with **red and yellow blazes** and a **blue horse symbol**
0.20	2.04	**R**	At fork onto thin singletrack. Head downhill on the **red and yellow blaze** trail
0.07	2.11	**R**	At three-way intersection as trail comes in from the left
0.03	2.14	**S**	Across a small wooden footbridge. Stay on the **yellow and red blaze** singletrack trail. Trail climbs back up the other side
0.11	2.25	**L**	At small gravel parking lot with **information board**
0.02	2.27	**BR**	Onto **yellow blaze** singletrack trail. Trail runs roughly parallel to the gravel road all the way up to the top of the hill
0.59	2.86	**S**	Across gravel road onto singletrack. Pass a gate onto the **red blaze** and **blue horse symbol** trail
0.12	2.98		After riding on a level ridge for awhile, the trail starts to go down a *fast, twisty, mild downhill*
0.20	3.18	**R**	At T intersection onto wider, dirt and gravel trail. Trail turns left and heads downhill. Pass **Area A campsite**. This is still the **red blaze** trail.
0.16	3.34	**S**	At **information board** at the end of the **red blaze** trail. Head up the bridle road (**blue blaze**)
0.16	3.50	**L**	Onto **yellow blaze** singletrack trail just before the gravel road intersection. The trail becomes a *fast, technical downhill*
0.24	3.74	**S**	At four-way intersection. Singletrack climbs back up other side
0.09	3.83		Trail begins a *long, twisty, technical, singletrack downhill*
0.10	3.93	**L**	At T intersection onto wider **green blaze** trail. Follow along the stream to the right
0.38	4.31	**S**	Across wooden footbridge over stream
0.06	4.37	**S**	Across wooden footbridge over stream
0.01	4.38	**L**	At three-way intersection. Singletrack trail begins long, technical climb
0.16	4.54	**L**	Top of climb. **Sunrise Lake** is down to the right. Turn **left** onto singletrack. Trail continues to climb

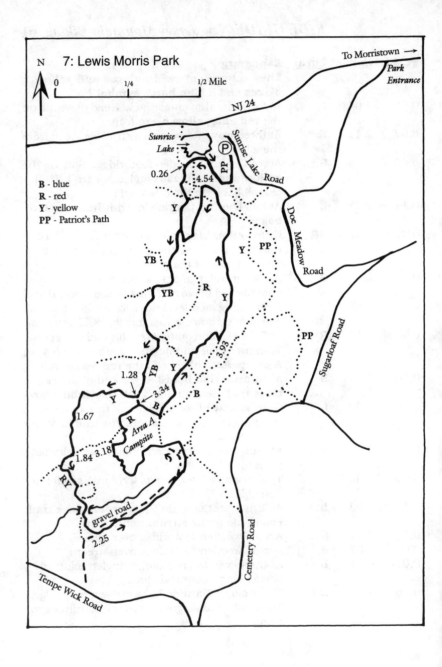

N

7: Lewis Morris Park

To Morristown →

Park Entrance

0   1/4   1/2 Mile

NJ 24

Sunrise Lake

Ⓟ

0.26   4.54

B - blue
R - red
Y - yellow
PP - Patriot's Path

Sunrise Lake Road

Doe Meadow Road

Y   PP

Y

YB

YB   R   Y

PP

3.93

Sugarloaf Road

YB   Y

1.28   3.34   B

1.67   R   B

Area A Campsite

1.84   3.18

RY

gravel road

2.25

Tempe Wick Road

Cemetery Road

Pt.-Pt.	Cume	Turn	Landmark
0.19	4.73	**SR**	Onto **blue blaze** trail. Trail begins *long, rocky, fast, technical downhill,* which will take you all the way back down to the pond
0.02	4.75	**S**	As **yellow blaze** trail comes in from the left
0.11	4.86	**BR**	As other fork drops off steeply to the left
0.06	4.92	**S**	Past a trail to the right
0.10	5.02	**L**	At a clearing just before the bottom of the hill
0.01	5.03	**R**	Onto the gravel road at the bottom of the hill. Follow gravel road around bends
0.15	5.18	**L**	Onto paved road, which goes uphill
0.09	5.27	**S**	Come out to parking lot and head downhill
0.02	5.29		Back to information board. End of route

Mahlon Dickerson Reservation—7.67 miles
Jefferson, Morris Co.

HIGHLIGHTS   ■ - ◆

TERRAIN:	Fairly rocky overall, with some very rocky sections
TOPOGRAPHY:	A number of long, extended climbs
DIFFICULTY:	Moderate to difficult
TRAIL TYPES:	Mostly singletrack, with some fire road and doubletrack

GENERAL INFORMATION

Mahlon Dickerson Reservation is a part of the Morris County Parks Commission. For more information contact:

> Morris County Parks Commission
> PO Box 1295
> Morristown, NJ 07062-1295
> (973) 326-7600

DIRECTIONS: Take Interstate 80 to Route 15 North. Take Rt. 15 north approximately five miles to the exit for Weldon Road. Follow Weldon Road northeast for about four miles to the Saffin Pond parking lot on the right. The reservation is on both sides of the road.

SIZE: About fifteen miles of trails on 3042 acres.

PARK HOURS: Dawn to dusk, year round.

ENTRY FEE: No charge.

TRAIL CLASSIFICATIONS: The trails at Mahlon Dickerson are not marked for difficulty. The trails in the northwestern section of the park are well marked, however, with white, blue, yellow, aqua and green blazes. The trails south and west of Weldon Road are all well marked with white or aqua blazes.

TRAIL MAPS: Trail maps are available at the directory at the RV/Trailer

Camping Area parking lot, and at the information board in the parking lot by the softball field.

RESTROOMS: There are restrooms at the RV camping area, across Weldon Road at the tent camping area, and at the parking lot by the softball field.

NEARBY MOUNTAIN BIKING AREAS: Allamuchy Mountain Park is about 15-20 miles west of Mahlon Dickerson, and Lewis Morris Park is about 20-25 miles southeast near Morristown.

OTHER PARK ACTIVITIES: Camping, picnicking, hiking, radio-controlled car racing and field archery are all popular at Mahlon Dickerson. There is fishing and ice skating at Saffin Pond. There is a softball field, and concerts are sometimes held at the reservation. Future additions may include an ice rink and the renovation of the former Ski Bowl alpine ski area.

OVERVIEW
Mahlon Dickerson is a rather large recreation area with an extensive trail system. There are a number of outstanding features in the park. From Headley Overlook, at 1300 feet above sea level, there is a beautiful scenic view of Bowling Green Mountain and Lake Hopatcong. There is a softball field, a radio- controlled race car track, picnic areas, camp sites for tents, RVs and trailers, and a defunct alpine ski area.

TERRAIN/TRAIL COMPOSITION: The trails at Mahlon Dickerson are fairly rocky. The park is located in a very hilly area, and a number of the climbs are long and grinding. Most of the trails are wide singletrack or thin, overgrown doubletrack, but there are some fire roads as well. The trails in the section north and west of Weldon Road contain more singletrack, and in general, are very technical and challenging. This section is the most popular for mountain biking. The trails get more usage and are maintained better than the more overgrown trails east of Weldon Road.

HISTORY: Mahlon Dickerson Reservation was dedicated in 1967. It is named after Mahlon Dickerson, a former Governor of New Jersey, a U.S. Senator, and Secretary of the Navy under two presidents. He lived from 1770 to 1840.

SPECIFIC TRAIL DIRECTIONS:
Advanced Loop: This loop encompasses much of the park, but concentrates on the better maintained, and in my opinion, more enjoyable section north and west of Weldon Road. The route begins and ends at the Saffin Pond parking lot in more or less the geographical center of the park. The majority of the route is comprised of something in between well-worn singletrack and overgrown doubletrack. In places, it is extremely rocky, and it is fairly rocky overall. Much of the terrain at the park is suitable for an intermediate-level rider, and the first half of this loop makes a sufficient route if you turn left instead of right at 3.06 miles and take Weldon Road back down to the parking lot.

Total route distance: 7.67 miles
Ride time for an advanced rider: 1.5-2.5 hours

Pt.-Pt.	Cume	Turn	Landmark
0.00	0.00	R	Come out of **Saffin Pond** parking lot and turn **right** onto **Weldon Road**
0.04	0.04	R	Onto first trail off the road. Overgrown doubletrack trail. After remaining level for awhile, the trail begins to climb
0.48	0.52	L	At three-way intersection as trail comes in from the right. The trail gets increasingly rocky as it continues to climb
0.24	0.76	R	Take the **right** fork. It leads down to a *loose, rocky downhill*
0.13	0.89	S	Across a wooden footbridge over a small stream at the bottom of the hill after crossing a technical rock garden. The trail then begins to climb again up a loose, rocky, technical hill
0.10	0.99	R	Follow the white blazes on the trees at the tent camping area. The trail continues to climb
0.12	1.11	S	Past the right turnoff for the white blaze trail
0.32	1.43	S	Past the right turnoff for the **Headley Overlook.** This is a very scenic overlook, and at close to 1300 feet above sea level, is a vantage point from which you can see miles and miles. The northern tip of **Lake**

Pt.-Pt.	Cume	Turn	Landmark
			Hopatcong is visible in the distance to the south
		S	The trail follows the aqua-colored paint blazes
0.11	1.54	S	Across **Weldon Road**. Pick up the singletrack trail directly across the road
0.12	1.66	R	At parking lot by the information board. Follow the parking lot to the end and take the paved path. Follow the white and aqua blazes and the signs for the **Pine Swamp Trail.** Pass a softball field on the left
0.12	1.78	S	At the end of the paved path onto a wide trail
0.09	1.87	R	Onto the **Pine Swamp Trail** (white blazes). The trail heads down a *fast, wide, rocky downhill*
0.10	1.97	L	At bottom of hill
0.21	2.18	R	Stay on the white and aqua blaze trail at three-way intersection
0.30	2.48	L	At three-way intersection. Get onto the **Boulder Trail** (green blazes)
0.02	2.50	S	Past the fork from the white blaze trail which comes in from the right. This section is fairly flat, but rocky
0.56	3.06	R	Onto white blaze trail at three-way intersection
0.01	3.07	R	At immediate three-way intersection. Stay on the **Pine Swamp Trail** (white blazes)
0.14	3.21	S	The trail traverses a swampy area before beginning a long, grinding climb. The trail gets very steep and then switchbacks to the left before taking on a milder approach to the climb
0.31	3.52	R	At a switchback turn to the right as a singletrack trail leads off to the left
0.04	3.56	S	Top of hill. There is a wooden bench on the left side of the trail and a sign on the right. This is the highest point in **Morris County** at 1395 feet above sea level
0.13	3.69	S	After remaining level for awhile, the trail

Pt.-Pt.	Cume	Turn	Landmark
			begins a *long, fast, loose-rocky, technical downhill,* which gets increasingly steeper and more technical
0.37	4.06	S	Across a rock garden at the bottom of the hill. The trail then begins to climb again
0.34	4.40	L	Take the **left** fork, the white blaze trail, which climbs up to the left. The right fork would be the yellow blaze trail
0.30	4.70	R	Right before the paved road, which is the boundary of the park. Follow the aqua blazes again
0.06	4.76	S	Come to the beginning of a series of technical rock gardens
0.04	4.80	S	Across a wooden footbridge
0.11	4.91	R	At three-way intersection. This is the beginning of the yellow blaze trail. This trail quickly thins down to singletrack
0.07	4.98	S	Across two-plank bridge over small stream. Cross through a swampy section with several planks laid down to make it a little bit easier to navigate
0.09	5.07	S	As the trail begins to climb. Pass a left turn for the blue trail. Stay on the yellow blaze trail, which climbs straight up a *rocky, technical, steep hill*
0.11	5.18	BL	Come back onto the white blaze trail. The trail eventually begins to climb back up towards the highest point in Morris County
0.45	5.63	R	Onto a narrower trail partway up the hill. This trail will become narrow, rocky doubletrack
0.33	5.96	S	Through a swampy section right in the midst of a rocky section
0.43	6.39	L	Onto the **Ogden Railroad Grade Trail.** This section is blazed with yellow and blue paint
0.32	6.71	S	Past a singletrack trail stemming off to the left
0.19	6.90	S	The railroad grade trail becomes an earth bridge between a swamp to the right and a

Pt.-Pt.	Cume	Turn	Landmark
			pond to the left
0.75	7.65	**S**	Across **Weldon Road** to **Saffin Pond parking lot**
0.02	7.67		Back to parking lot. End of route

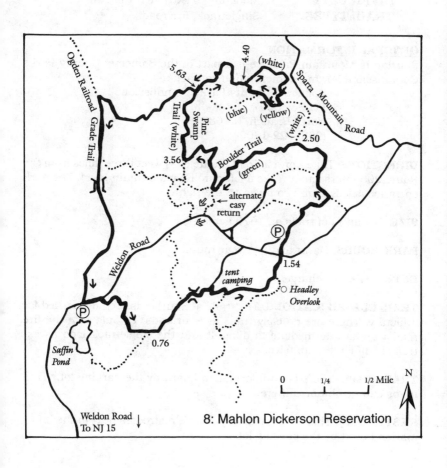

8: Mahlon Dickerson Reservation

Sourlands Mountain Preserve—4.19 miles
Hillsborough & Montgomery Townships, Somerset Co.

HIGHLIGHTS ■■ - ◆◆

TERRAIN: Extremely rocky, rooty
TOPOGRAPHY: Big hills: long and steep
DIFFICULTY: Moderate to extremely difficult
TRAIL TYPES: Singletrack, fire road

GENERAL INFORMATION

Sourlands Mountain Preserve is a part of the Somerset County Parks Commission. For more information contact:

Somerset County Parks Commission
PO Box 5327
North Branch, NJ 08876
(908) 722-1200

DIRECTIONS: Take Amwell Road (Route 514) west three miles from the Route 206 intersection. Take a left onto East Mountain Road. The park entrance is less than two miles on the right.

SIZE: Six miles of trails on 1670 acres.

PARK HOURS: Dawn to dusk, year round.

ENTRY FEE: No charge

TRAIL CLASSIFICATIONS: The trails at Sourlands are not marked for difficulty. There are no easy trails at Sourlands. I would rate the fire road trail as intermediate to difficult and the singletrack loop as extremely difficult to abusive.

TRAIL MAPS: There is an information board by the parking lot. Trail maps can be obtained there.

RESTROOMS: There are a pair of portable restrooms next to the information board by the parking lot.

NEARBY MOUNTAIN BIKING AREAS: Round Valley Recreation Area is ten to fifteen miles northwest of Sourlands, but no areas are very close.

OTHER PARK ACTIVITIES: Hiking.

OVERVIEW

Sourlands Mountain Preserve is owned by Somerset County and administered by the Somerset County Parks Commission. The parks commission strives to provide passive control to create an undisturbed natural setting. There are no facilities at the preserve and the area has been left in its original condition as much as possible. Several wooden bridges linking the main trail between some of the rockier sections are the only man-made structures at Sourlands. Sourlands is located on the side of the Sourland Mountain Range. The parking lot is on the valley floor and the back of the park is at the top of the ridge.

While mountain biking is not officially allowed at the preserve, all trails are designated as multi-use; mountain bikes are not specifically prohibited according to the park rules and regulations. The parks commission is addressing the issue and working on a plan to create a separate area for mountain biking in the future.

There are two primary trails at Sourlands. One is a fire road trail following a pipeline which divides the developed part of the preserve in half. It is the less technical of the trails, but following the pipeline straight up the side of the mountain provides an intense, steep, long climb up from the valley floor or a fast and loose downhill on the return. The other trail is a longer loop which is defined by the Somerset County Parks Commission as thirteen separate interconnecting trails starting and ending at the parking lot and traveling in a counter-clockwise direction. Starting at the parking lot on trail #1 you normally must stay right at every intersection to stay on the loop. Taking a left at any intersection will cut off the loop and head you back toward the parking lot.

TERRAIN/TRAIL COMPOSITION: Aside from the fire road trail, which is less rocky and wide open, all of the trails are extremely rocky, twisty singletrack. There are several stretches on the loop where there are 100 feet or more of largely impassable rock gardens. The southern half of the loop (mainly from trail 7 to 10) is somewhat less rocky, but overall it is about as rocky and rough as mountain biking in New Jersey can get.

After nearly an hour-long ride of four and a half miles, I am usually battered enough to be ready to go home. The loop trail is very slow going and can be frustrating. There are numerous sections which are so rocky that they can best be cleared by using trials techniques. If you are a fan of extremely rocky, technical riding, then definitely give Sourlands a try.

SPECIFIC TRAIL DIRECTIONS:

Advanced to Abusive Loop: This route doesn't seem very long on paper at just over four miles, but it contains about four miles of the roughest, rockiest, most frustrating, technically demanding terrain I've ever ridden. Most of the route looks like a war zone, with large, irregularly shaped rocks and numerous fallen logs only occasionally speckled with short, smooth patches. And if that isn't enough, the entire trail system is on the side of a long ridge. The route climbs over 350 vertical feet in the first mile until it levels out at the top of the ridge. Although it may seem sadomasochistic, this route can be exhilarating if you are an expert rider and everything is clicking. If you start the ride, but then feel as though you've gotten in over your head, turn left at trail marker #1, #3 or #5 for a quick run back to the parking lot.

Total route distance: 4.19 miles
Ride time for an advanced rider: 1.0-1.5 hours

Pt.-Pt.	Cume	Turn	Landmark
0.00	0.00	S	From the parking lot ride straight across the field past the **information board** to the trailhead
0.04	0.04	S	Trail becomes singletrack. Follow signs throughout route marked with a rectangle
0.06	0.10	S	Trail begins **long, grinding climb**
0.04	0.14	S	Cross wooden footbridge
0.08	0.22	S	Cross two more wooden footbridges
0.06	0.28	R	Follow arrow on **trail marker #1** and continue to climb
0.12	0.40	S	At non-intersection. Follow the arrow on **trail marker #2**. Still climbing
0.05	0.45	R	At **trail marker #3** and climb some more. This section is **very rocky and difficult to navigate**

Pt.-Pt.	Cume	Turn	Landmark
0.16	0.61	**S**	Cross stream
0.16	0.77	**S**	Several log crossings. Trail levels out
0.14	0.91	**L**	At **trail marker #4**. Trail starts to go mildly downhill
0.18	1.09	**S**	At rocky stream crossing. This is followed by **the first excessively difficult rock garden**
0.03	1.12	**S**	Cross wooden footbridge and navigate another rock garden
0.07	1.19	**S**	At **trail marker #5**. Trail comes out into clearing at the top of the **pipeline**
0.02	1.21	**R/L**	Onto pipeline doubletrack trail. Cross a stream and make an immediate **left** onto singletrack
0.04	1.25	**S**	Re-enter the woods. Cross a wooden footbridge
0.03	1.28	**BR**	Be careful to stay on the trail, which goes right across a small rocky stream crossing. The trail looks like it continues straight ahead, but if you do not bear right, the trail dies in about fifty feet. As a landmark, there is a wooden footbridge ahead and to the right
0.04	1.32	**S**	Across that wooden footbridge and then another one. **This section is very rocky**
0.10	1.42	**S**	Cross a wooden footbridge and then a very long wooden footbridge
0.18	1.60	**S**	*Very technical downhill combined with a rock garden. Watch out!*
0.14	1.74	**L**	At **trail marker #6**. The trail follows along a chain link fence. This is *an extremely steep and rocky, but short, downhill.* I find it much easier to keep from going over the handlebars if I get back behind my saddle and rest my chest on it. The topmost portion is extremely steep, but fairly smooth. Then, as the trail comes back to a more ridable angle, **it gets very rocky**
0.31	2.05	**R**	At **trail marker #7**. The trail marker is not facing your direction. Ignore the arrow and turn **right**
0.20	2.25	**L**	At **trail marker #8**.
0.19	2.44	**L**	Onto singletrack. Straight takes you out to a field. This section of trail is a lot of fun. **It is**

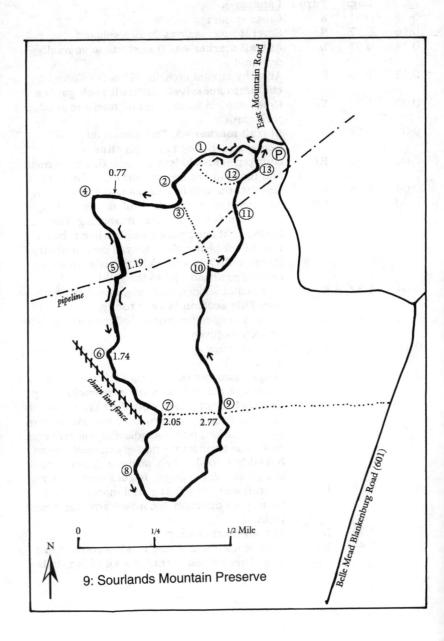

East Mountain Road

① ⑫ ⑬ Ⓟ

0.77
② ④ ③ ⑪

⑤ 1.19
⑩

pipeline

⑥ 1.74

chain link fence

⑦ ⑨
2.05 2.77

⑧

0   1/4   1/2 Mile

N

9: Sourlands Mountain Preserve

Belle Mead Blankenburg Road (601)

Pt.-Pt.	Cume	Turn	Landmark
			twisty and smooth, with nicely contoured, banked turns and several small stream crossings. One of the only sections on this route which is possible to ride fast
0.30	2.74	**S**	Cross a wooden footbridge
0.03	2.77	**S**	At four-way intersection at **trail marker #9**. Do not follow the arrow on the trail marker
0.68	3.45	**R**	At **trail marker #10**
0.42	3.87	**S**	At **trail marker #11**. Re-cross the **pipeline trail**, go straight across a wooden footbridge and back into the woods
0.14	4.01	**R**	Follow the arrow on **trail marker #12**
0.04	4.05	**S**	Come out into clearing and follow this trail down and back into the woods to the left. Cross a rocky stream
0.08	4.13	**S**	Come out of the woods at **trail marker #13**, which is aptly marked "END." The parking lot is straight across the clearing and a little to the left
0.06	4.19		Back to parking lot. End of route

Washington Valley Park (White Rock)— 4.80/8.41 miles

Martinsville, Somerset Co.

HIGHLIGHTS ■ - ◆◆

TERRAIN: Relatively smooth to very rocky

TOPOGRAPHY: Several longer hills, some flatter twisty sections

DIFFICULTY: Moderate to extremely difficult

TRAIL TYPES: Lots of twisty singletrack, limited fire road

GENERAL INFORMATION

Chimney Rock Park is a part of the Somerset County Parks Commission. For more information contact:

Somerset County Parks Commission
PO Box 5327
North Branch, NJ 08876
(908) 722-1200

DIRECTIONS: Take I-287 to Rt. 22 East. Turn right at the first exit for Thompson Ave./Bound Brook/Martinsville. Take the immediate right jughandle for Martinsville and cross over Rt. 22. Turn left at the stop sign. Follow the road as it winds its way up through a gorge. After the road levels out, Chimney Rock Park will be on the right. Park here for the grand tour loop. For the western route continue past the park and turn left at the T. Turn left onto Newman's Lane in half a mile. Take Newman's Lane down and across a narrow bridge. Park in the small (four cars maximum) parking lot on the right before you go up the long hill.

SIZE: Fifteen to twenty miles of trails on approximately 1500 to 2000 acres.

PARK HOURS: Dawn to dusk, year round.

ENTRY FEE: No charge.

TRAIL CLASSIFICATIONS: The Somerset County Parks Commission has no classification system of its own for the park. The western section contains sections of roller-coaster-esque, smooth singletrack as well as very technical, rocky, twisting singletrack with an excessive number of loose-rocky sections. The eastern section contains longer, steeper, grinding climbs and descents, with even more loose-rocky sections thrown in for good measure.

TRAIL MAPS: None exist.

RESTROOMS: There are no facilities at the park.

NEARBY MOUNTAIN BIKING AREAS: Sourlands Mountain Preserve is about fifteen miles south. Round Valley is about fifteen miles west.

OTHER PARK ACTIVITIES: Hiking, fishing, baseball, basket-ball, snowmobiling and cross-country skiing.

OVERVIEW
The riding at White Rock is based around the Chimney Rock Park, which is a small, outdoor-sport-based park on Chimney Rock Road in Martinsville. This park acts as a hub, from which singletrack trails extend in several directions.

TERRAIN/TRAIL COMPOSITION: The terrain at White Rock is very rocky. Where there are hills (the eastern and western sections), the hills are big and long, and excessively rocky. The central connecting section of the park is less rocky and relatively flatter, but there are still patches of rocky terrain and short but ferocious hills.

The trails are almost entirely singletrack, rocky and extremely twisty in nature. There are numerous sections where the trail will take a tight 270-degree turn before heading off in a completely different direction. Trails at White Rock spring up with a surprising regularity. At this point, there are about twenty miles of trails, but I would imagine that the trail system will look a lot different in a year's time.

HISTORY: White Rock is a fairly new area for mountain biking. Trails began to spring up all over the park around the same time that I first found out that biking was an allowable activity there in the spring of 1995. There is not much of a history to the park. The western section borders an active rock quarrying operation, and there are several trails which wind back and forth across the remnants of a few ancient stone boundary walls.

SPECIFIC TRAIL DIRECTIONS: There are two routes for White Rock/ Chimney Rock/Washington Valley Park. The first is a five-mile route that twists and turns its way all over the western section. It is a figure eight, which splits up nicely into two halves. The second route is longer and more demanding. It encompasses all of the sections of the park and the highlights of the most technical aspects of White Rock. At less than eight miles, it is deceptively long. The loop covers a lot of ground, and it feels like a much longer route than the mileage would have you believe.

Advanced Western Loop: Starting, finishing, and passing through the small parking lot at the bottom of the hill on Newman's Lane.

Total route distance: 4.80 miles
Ride time for an advanced rider: 1.0-1.5 hours

Pt.-Pt.	Cume	Turn	Landmark
0.0	0.00	**S**	Begin to ride uphill on **Newman's Lane**
0.04	0.04	**R**	Onto first singletrack turnoff. Cross a few logs
0.07	0.11	**BL**	After remaining level for awhile, the trail starts a **long, steep, rocky singletrack climb**
0.22	0.33		Trail starts to dip downward for a short stretch. Very twisty
0.05	0.38		Trail starts to climb again, but at a much more relaxed pace. Trail becomes increasingly rocky and technical. After a stream crossing there is a **short, very steep, loose-rocky, technical climb** followed by a less steep, but just as technical, climb
0.14	0.52	**BL**	Pass the right turn at the three-way intersection. Trail levels out
0.21	0.73	**R**	At three-way intersection. Immediate left

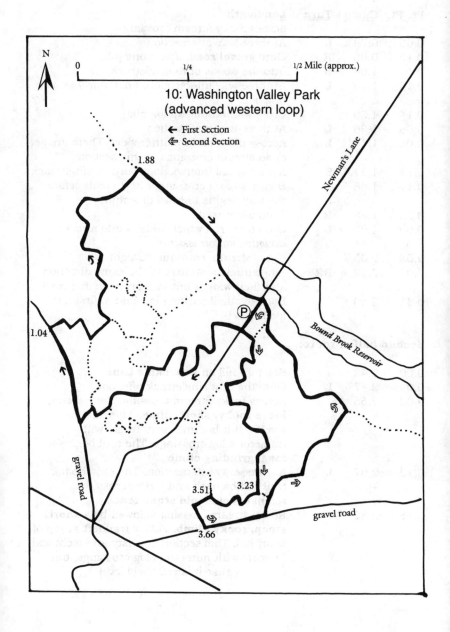

N

0   1/4   1/2 Mile (approx.)

10: Washington Valley Park
(advanced western loop)

← First Section
⇐ Second Section

Newman's Lane

1.88

↰

↗

Ⓟ ↶

⇩

1.04

Bound Brook Reservoir

↰

↓

⇦

gravel road

⇩

↗

3.51   3.23

⇦

gravel road

3.66

PtPt.	Cume	Turn	Landmark
			across rocky stream crossing
0.05	0.78	**L**	At three-way intersection
0.12	0.90	**R**	Onto **gravel road** after stone pile
0.14	1.04	**R**	Into the woods onto singletrack
0.12	1.16	**L**	At three-way intersection. *Fast, fairly smooth downhill*
0.14	1.30		Cross a tall, built-up log pile
0.06	1.36	**L**	At three-way intersection
0.08	1.44	**L**	Across ditch and up other side. There are six or so stream crossings in this section
0.13	1.57	**S**	Across small intersection. Stay on singletrack
0.11	1.68		Bigger stream crossing. Short climb before the trail begins to head downhill
0.20	1.88	**R**	Onto wider trail
0.09	1.97	**L**	Onto thin trail which widens into a *rocky downhill multitrack trail*
0.08	2.05		Cross stream, continue straight
0.07	2.12	**BR**	Singletrack continues in the same direction and then widens out into primitive fire road
0.31	2.43		Back to small parking lot. End of first half of loop

Second half of route:

0.00	2.43		Start up hill on **Newman's Lane**
0.04	2.47	**L**	Onto the first singletrack offshoot
0.08	2.55		Across rocky stream crossing. **Very steep, loose-rocky, short climb.** After the trail levels out it becomes very twisty with numerous log crossings. The trail begins a **long, grinding climb**
0.12	2.67	**L**	At three-way intersection. The switchback trail climbs back and forth across the remnants of an **old stone fence**
0.15	2.82		Rocky stream crossing followed by a **short, steep, rocky climb.** Follow trail **left** at top of short hill. This section is twisty and technical in spots with numerous log crossings, but faster because it is relatively level

Pt.-Pt.	Cume	Turn	Landmark
0.17	2.99	**S**	Rocky stream crossing. **Straight** across stream. There are numerous log crossings on this next section
0.16	3.15		Trail starts to climb. More log crossings
0.08	3.23	**BR**	At three-way intersection up **short, steep climb.** More log crossings
0.10	3.33	**BR**	Cross tall, built-up log pile. Stay on singletrack
0.03	3.36	**R**	Into woods on singletrack. More log crossings
0.14	3.50	**R**	After sharp right turn in trail, ride across a **rocky, technical stream crossing**
0.01	3.51	**L**	At T intersection. Still singletrack
0.15	3.66	**L**	Onto gravel fire road
0.17	3.83	**S**	At multiple intersection onto dirt doubletrack road. The trail starts *a very fast, loose-rocky, technical fire road downhill*
0.16	3.99	**BL**	Stay on semi-gravel doubletrack at fork
0.08	4.07	**BR**	At fork. Trail makes a sharp right turn. Continue downhill
0.12	4.19	**BL**	At fork
0.12	4.31	**L**	After stream crossing at top of ditch
0.22	4.53		Rocky, technical stream crossing
0.04	4.57		*Short, extremely rocky downhill section.* Cross stream and climb back up other side to level ground
0.14	4.71		Another rocky stream crossing
0.06	4.77	**BR**	Trail leads you around fence
0.03	4.80		Back to small parking lot. End of route

Advanced Grand Tour Loop: This loop starts and ends at the Chimney Rock Park parking lot. It is a deceptively long ride, even at less than ten miles. This loop encompasses all of the sections of the park: the Eastern White Rock section, the Western section and all of the intermediary sections between Chimney Rock Road and Newman's Lane. This is an advanced loop which tends to become abusive in spots.

Total route distance: 8.41 miles
Ride time for an advanced rider: 2.0-3.0 hours

Pt.-Pt.	Cume	Turn	Landmark
0.00	0.00		From the parking lot, ride away from **Chimney Rock Road**. Pass the tennis courts and cross the basketball court area. Head out off the back corner of the plateau that the basketball court is on towards the far right corner of the park
0.25	0.25	**S**	Trailhead. Enter a singletrack trail that immediately goes down an *extremely rocky, steep, technical, but short hill*
0.05	0.30	**BR**	On the other side of a rocky stream crossing
0.08	0.38	**R**	At a fork. The trail winds its way to a **very technical, tricky stream crossing** and up to a road
0.06	0.44	**L**	Onto paved road. After crossing a bridge, the road begins a **long climb**
0.26	0.70	**BR**	Near the top of the hill onto a singletrack trail
0.02	0.72	**R**	Straight down a *steep little hill*
0.01	0.73		Another **very rocky, technical stream crossing** followed by a **long, steep, extremely rocky climb**
0.08	0.81	**L**	At three-way intersection onto another singletrack
0.04	0.85		After crossing a small stream and the remnants of an old stone fence, cross a very tall, built-up log pile
0.19	1.04	**L**	At a fork
0.17	1.21	**S**	At three-way intersection past a left turn. Trail gets wider
0.06	1.27	**R**	Onto singletrack off of wider trail. This

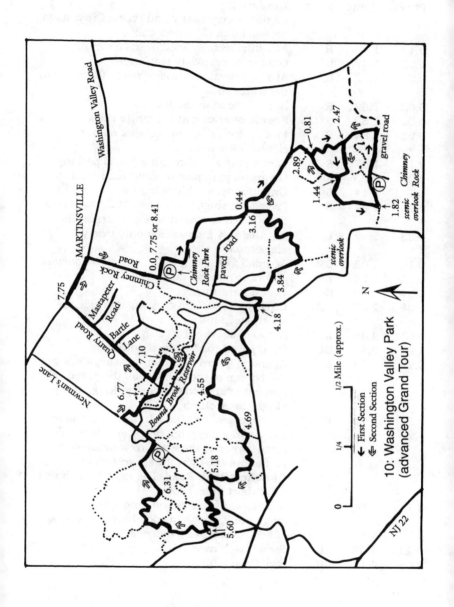

10: Washington Valley Park (advanced Grand Tour)

Pt.-Pt.	Cume	Turn	Landmark
			section is very twisty and rocky. Cross a long portion of an old stone wall
0.17	1.44	**R**	At T intersection. Trail heads downhill
0.03	1.47	**L**	Onto thinner, twisty singletrack
0.25	1.72	**L**	At T intersection onto fire road. Climb up to the **white rock**
0.08	1.80	**R**	At a left bend in the fire road
0.02	1.82		**Scenic overlook** at the **white rock**
0.02	1.84	**R**	From the overlook to get back onto the climbing fire road
0.13	1.97	**S**	Pass a gate and through a gravel parking lot
0.06	2.03	**S**	On gravel road past a gravel road right turn
0.11	2.14	**L**	Onto thinner multitrack trail
0.10	2.24	**S**	Pass a left singletrack turn. Multitrack trail thins down to singletrack as it descends
0.23	2.47	**L**	At three-way intersection onto twisty singletrack
0.16	2.63	**BR**	At small fork. *Fast, rocky, technical downhill*
0.15	2.78	**BR**	At fork to stay on main trail
0.01	2.79	**S**	Pass a right turn
0.08	2.87		Cross rocky stream crossing and ride up short, steep hill
0.01	2.88	**L**	At top of short hill
0.01	2.89	**BL**	Onto paved road. Take it downhill
0.27	3.16	**L**	At end of **guard rail** after crossing a bridge at the bottom of the hill. Get off the paved road and onto **very twisty, rocky, long, steep singletrack climb**
0.54	3.70	**R**	At T intersection. The left turn would take you down a steep hill to a scenic overlook catty-corner to the white rock overlook, and just above the tight, twisty section of **Chimney Rock Road**. The right turn climbs for a short time
0.14	3.84	**L**	At four-way intersection onto another singletrack, which quickly becomes a *rocky, rutted, steep, twisty downhill*
0.23	4.07	**SL**	Switchback turn
0.05	4.12	**SR**	Switchback turn

Pt.-Pt.	Cume	Turn	Landmark
0.02	4.14	**L**	Onto **Chimney Rock Road**
0.04	4.18	**SR**	Across the road around the end of a chainlink fence onto a rocky singletrack along the western boundary of the reservoir
0.11	4.29	**S**	After widening out to a rocky fire road, continue straight past a left fork which heads uphill. **Stay along the shoreline of the reservoir.** Eventually, the fire road turns away from the reservoir and begins a **long, grinding, rocky, technical climb**
0.26	4.55	**L**	At intersection with another rocky fire road. A right turn would quickly take you down and out to the small parking lot on Newman's Lane. The **left** turn continues to climb
0.14	4.69	**SR**	Onto singletrack just before a five-way fire road intersection
0.02	4.71	**L**	Onto another singletrack
0.13	4.84		After a right turn in the trail, you will come to a rocky, technical stream crossing
0.01	4.85	**R**	At a T intersection. The trail is rocky singletrack with numerous technical log pile crossings
0.21	5.06		Long rocky stream crossing at the bottom of a very small hill
0.12	5.18	**L**	At three-way intersection. Pass an enormous fallen tree and cross a technical, rocky, rutted stream bed
0.12	5.30	**S**	Diagonally across **Newman's Lane** to singletrack trail on other side
0.13	5.43		Cross a tall, built-up log pile
0.13	5.56	**L**	At three-way intersection. Trail immediately bears left across a rocky stream crossing
0.04	5.60	**R**	At three-way intersection
0.10	5.70	**R**	At three-way intersection. This section is a *mild, relatively smooth, twisty, singletrack downhill*
0.15	5.85		Cross a tall, built-up log pile
0.05	5.90	**L**	At three-way intersection
0.08	5.98	**BR**	At fork. There are numerous small stream

Pt.-Pt.	Cume	Turn	Landmark
			crossings in this section
0.33	6.31	L	At T intersection onto a wider trail. The trail quickly becomes a *very fast and loose downhill.* There is a rocky compression ditch at the bottom of the hill
0.08	6.39	BR	Wider trail continues to the right
0.12	6.51	L	Come out to the small parking lot on **Newman's Lane**. Turn **left** onto the road and cross the bridge
0.13	6.64	R	Onto singletrack at end of guardrail for the bridge
0.04	6.68	L	Onto fire road heading away from Newman's Lane
0.08	6.76	L	Onto thinner trail after deep, rocky, technical stream crossing
0.01	6.77	R	Onto uphill singletrack
0.02	6.79	R	Onto another singletrack immediately after a log pile
0.17	6.96	S	At intersection for wider trail. Stay on singletrack
0.14	7.10	L	After a ditch, the trail turns left and drops you onto another single track. Turn left and head in the opposite direction from the trail you were just on
0.11	7.21	R	At four-way intersection onto wider singletrack trail
0.07	7.28	BL	At three-way intersection. Stay on main trail
0.02	7.30	R	At three-way intersection
0.02	7.32	L	Onto gravel road (end section of Quarry Road)
0.07	7.39	S	Pass a doubletrack road on the right
0.07	7.46	S	Pass **Bartle Lane.** Quarry Road is paved from this intersection out to Washington Valley Road.
0.09	7.55	S	Pass **Mastapeter Road**
0.20	7.75	R	Onto **Washington Valley Road**
0.21	7.96	R	Onto **Chimney Rock Road**
0.40	8.36	L	At entrance for **Chimney Rock Park**
0.05	8.41		Back to parking lot. End of route

Delaware & Raritan Canal State Park—
28.02 miles/8.33 miles
New Brunswick - Lambertville

HIGHLIGHTS

TERRAIN:	**Smooth hardpack, some roots**
TOPOGRAPHY:	**Flat**
DIFFICULTY:	**Recreational, easy**
TRAIL TYPES:	**Multitrack**

GENERAL INFORMATION
The Delaware and Raritan Canal is a part of the New Jersey State Park Service. For more information contact:

Delaware and Raritan Canal State Park
643 Canal Road
Somerset, NJ 08873
(732) 873-3050

DIRECTIONS: The canal path follows the Raritan River from New Brunswick to Trenton, where it then follows the Delaware River up to Stockton. There are dozens of places to get onto the path.

SIZE: Fifty miles of trails.

PARK HOURS: Dawn to dusk, year round.

ENTRY FEE: No charge.

TRAIL CLASSIFICATIONS: The canal path is flat and relatively smooth. On the Raritan River portion north of Amwell Road in Millstone, the path has more exposed roots, and in general is not as smooth a ride as the rest of the trail. The vast remainder of the trail is suitable for hybrids and even some sturdy road touring bikes.

TRAIL MAPS: Trail maps are posted at every major road intersection.

RESTROOMS: The only facilities are at Washington Crossing State Park and Bulls Island State Park on the Delaware River portion of the trail.

NEARBY MOUNTAIN BIKING AREAS: Mercer County Park and Sourlands Mountain Preserve are both near sections of the canal trail.

OTHER PARK ACTIVITIES: Walking, running, camping, fishing.

OVERVIEW
The Delaware and Raritan Canal Trail is a great place to ride on many levels. As a continuous route from end to end, it is the closest thing to an epic off-road journey that New Jersey has to offer. As a ten to twenty mile section, it can be a day-long outing at a relaxed pace. And with the numerous points of interest and historical markers along the way, it can be an educational and enjoyable experience for a family trip without needing a car.

HISTORY: The canals along the Delaware and Raritan Rivers were the major trade routes across New Jersey from their completion in 1834 until the 1930s, when other forms of transportation made canal travel obsolete. The tow paths which ran along either side of the canals were used by mules, which pulled the coal-laden barges along the canal from Pennsylvania to New York. Originally, there were fourteen locks along the canal system to raise and lower boat traffic.

The Raritan leg of the canal path has become one of the first official parts of the proposed Greenway Alliance trail. The trail, when completed, will mirror the Appalachian Trail from Georgia to Maine, travelling through all of the major urban areas along the Atlantic. It will be entirely accessible by bike.

TERRAIN/TRAIL COMPOSITION: In general, the trail is a flat, smooth, straight and wide dirt road. The composition varies from area to area, however. Along the Delaware River, the trail is wide and well maintained. Once you get outside the city of Trenton, it consists of a fine, hard-packed gravel that is very smooth. Along the Raritan River, the trail composition is less consistent. For the first ten or fifteen miles from the northeastern end of the trail in New Brunswick, it is a combination of gravel and sand, with numerous roots growing across the path. Further south, there are fewer roots, and the trail becomes a dirt doubletrack. Near Princeton, it is better maintained, with a wider, smoother, fine

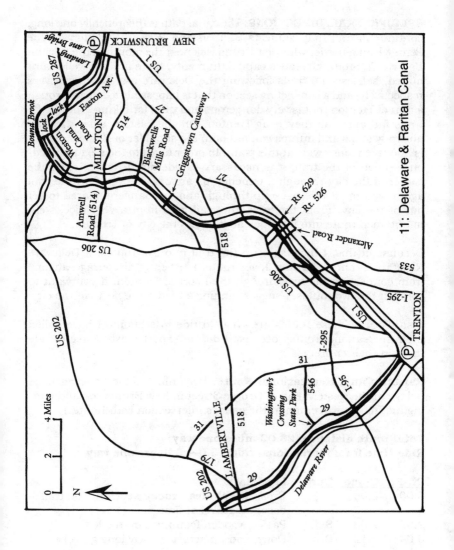

11: Delaware & Raritan Canal

gravel surface. The terrain is flat for the most part. There are a number of small hills around certain inconsistencies and man-made structures.

SPECIFIC TRAIL DIRECTIONS: The canal path is theoretically one long, continuous trail that connects Bull's Island Park in Stockton on the Pennsylvania border with New Brunswick near the mouth of the Raritan Bay via Trenton, the state's capital. In reality, there are two well-maintained, safe, scenic trails following the Delaware and Raritan Rivers respectively, and a connecting section that is impossible to follow through a part of Trenton that is very dangerous and unfit for biking. Both of the trails fall apart as they near Trenton. On the eastern side, the trail abruptly stops and dumps you out onto the shoulder of Route 1, which is about ten lanes wide at this point. In order to get to the next mapped-out section of the trail, it is necessary to ride down Route 1 into the center of the city through a treacherous area. Once you find the trail again, you must ride back up through another dangerous area to get out of the city. From the west, the trail goes from a very nice, well-maintained route into pure hell as it enters the city of Trenton.

Because of this, I have split up the trail into two routes: a Delaware River route and a Raritan River route. I fervently discourage anyone from connecting the two through the heart of Trenton. If you want to connect the two routes, I suggest finding a road route north of the city.

Also, both of these routes are great to ride in sections. I have called them recreational routes because I do not expect most people to ride them in their entirety.

Raritan Canal Recreational Route: Beginning at the Landing Lane Bridge at the western end of George Street in New Brunswick and ending just north of Trenton at the canal's intersection with Route 1.

Total route distance: 28.02 miles one way
Ride time for a recreational rider: 3.0-4.0 hours one way

Pt.-Pt.	Cume	Turn	Landmark
0.00	0.00		Cross a **technical, rocky section**. The trail becomes gravel at first
2.03	2.03	S	Pass a wooden footbridge on the left
0.09	2.12	S	Down and up across a fairly long gravel em

Pt.-Pt.	Cume	Turn	Landmark
			bankment section
1.42	3.54	S	Cross under the bridge for **Interstate 287** for the first time
0.10	3.64	S	Pass a wooden bridge over a lock to the left. There is a small dirt parking lot on the other side of the lock
1.38	5.02	S	At four-way intersection. Pass an old railroad bridge on the left
0.19	5.21	S	Across street in **South Bound Brook**. Pass a lock on the left on the other side of the street
0.51	5.72	S	Down and up across a concrete spillway
0.45	6.17	S	Cross under the bridge for **Interstate 287** for the second time. The trail becomes a rooty dirt doubletrack
1.19	7.36	S	Pass a concrete footbridge on the left
0.01	7.37	S	Pass a pump house building on the right
0.01	7.38	S	Across a lock
0.60	7.98	S	Across a paved entrance road for a private school
0.56	8.54	S	Across **Weston Canal Road**
1.99	10.53	S	Cross **Amwell Road (Rt. 514)** after passing through a small parking lot in **Millstone**. This section is smoother, primarily dirt with interspersed grass
2.09	12.62	S	Cross **Blackwells Mills Road**. Pass a parking lot on the right
1.75	14.37	S	Across a rocky gravel area
0.98	15.35	S	Cross **Griggstown Causeway**
0.02	15.37	S	Pass a wooden footbridge
0.27	15.64	S	Across a gravel road with a small bridge to the right and to the left
0.32	15.96	S	Small down and up across a long stone em bankment
1.02	16.98	S	Cross a wooden bridge at a four-way intersection
1.00	17.98	S	Across **Route 518**. Pass the Kingston stone refinery on the left
1.75	19.73	R	Follow sign for tunnel for tow path under **Route 27**

Pt.-Pt.	Cume	Turn	Landmark
0.09	19.82	S	Across paved road. Pass a lock on the left
0.31	20.13	S	Cross to the right side of the canal. The path becomes wide and smooth. The river has been dammed up to create a lake wide and calm enough for sailboats
1.95	22.08	S	Cross wooden footbridge over canal
0.02	22.10	S	Walk bike across wooden bridge as canal crosses over part of the river
0.39	22.49	S	Across **Route 629**
0.64	23.13	S	Across **Route 526**
0.39	23.52	S	Cross under a railroad bridge
0.04	23.56	S	Across **Alexander Road**. Pass a gravel parking lot on the other side of the road. The path is sandy in this section. Pass a park on the right
0.57	24.13	S	Path narrows down to singletrack
0.87	25.00	S	Pass a golf course on the right
0.15	25.15	S	Golf course is now on both sides of the trail
0.09	25.24	S	Pass a wooden footbridge to the left
0.53	25.77	L	Stay on trail to the **left** as it comes to a bend in a road
0.35	26.12	S	Cross road
0.24	26.36	L	Take the **left** fork that leads underneath the road
1.35	27.71	S	Cross under **Interstate 295**
0.11	27.82	S	Cross under another bridge
0.20	28.02	X	Come out into dirt parking lot. End of route. To get back to the starting point, follow the directions in reverse

Delaware Canal Recreational Route: This route starts in northwest Trenton and heads northwest along the Delaware River and Pennsylvania border all the way up to Lambertville and New Hope. In general, it is smoother and more even than the Raritan River branch.

Total route distance: 8.33 miles one way
Ride time for a recreational rider: 1.0-1.5 hours one way

Pt.-Pt.	Cume	Turn	Landmark
0.00	0.00		Beginning from Wilburtha Road, head

PtPt.	Cume	Turn	Landmark
			northwest away from Trenton. This section of trail is well-maintained, smooth gravel
0.46	0.46	**S**	Across **Route 175**
0.41	0.87	**S**	Cross under **Interstate 95**
0.25	1.12	**S**	Cross under another road. The **Delaware River** is down to the left
0.12	1.24	**S**	Pass the road for **Delaware & Raritan State Park**, **Scudder's Falls** parking area
0.46	1.70	**S**	Across spillway for overflow water
0.46	2.16	**S**	Across road for bridge across the **Delaware River** at **Washington's Crossing**. **Washington's Crossing State Park** is on both sides of the trail
1.00	3.16	**S**	Across paved road
0.05	3.21	**S**	Cross **Church Road**
0.64	3.85	**S**	Across paved road
1.61	5.46	**S**	Across bridge
0.29	5.75	**S**	Pass an old, broken-down railroad drawbridge across the canal itself
0.40	6.15	**S**	Cross a dirt bridge across an overflow spillway into the **Delaware River**
0.29	6.44	**S**	Pass a wooden footbridge across the canal on the right
0.55	6.99	**S**	Across a gravel road
0.07	7.06	**S**	Pass a water flow regulator on the **Delaware River**
0.22	7.28	**R**	Cross over the canal across a lock to the right side. Trail is hard-packed sand
0.19	7.47	**S**	Across a wooden footbridge. Pass a small playground on the right. Enter **Lambertville**
0.15	7.62	**S**	Cross wooden footbridge over tall dam
0.12	7.74	**S**	Cross **Bridge Street**. Ride down boardwalk ramp to trail on other side of street
0.12	7.86	**S**	Cross **Coryell Street**. Trail becomes singletrack along river before widening back to multitrack
0.47	8.33	**X**	There is construction on the canal path. It does not start again for several miles. This is the end of this route. To get back to the start, follow the directions in reverse

Cheesequake State Park—3.60 miles
Matawan, Middlesex Co.

HIGHLIGHTS ∎

TERRAIN:	Some roots, multiple log crossings
TOPOGRAPHY:	Roller-coaster-esque, with a few longer hills
DIFFICULTY:	Intermediate
TRAIL TYPES:	Mostly singletrack, with some connecting fire road

GENERAL INFORMATION
Cheesequake State Park is a part of the New Jersey Division of Parks and Forestry. For more information contact:

> Cheesequake State Park
> Matawan, NJ 07747
> (732) 566-2161

DIRECTIONS: From the Garden State Parkway, take exit 120 onto south-bound Laurence Harbor Parkway. Turn right onto Cliffwood Ave. Turn right onto Gordon Road and follow it into the park entrance. After going through the toll booth, continue straight and park in the first parking lot on the left.

From Route 34 East, turn left onto Morristown Road, which eventually turns into Gordon Road. Enter the park at the end of Gordon Road and continue straight after passing through the toll booth. Park in the first parking lot on the left.

SIZE: Fifteen to twenty miles of trails on 1274 acres. However, bikes are only allowed on the multi-use trail, which is about three miles long.

PARK HOURS: 8 a.m. to 6 p.m. (open until 8 p.m. during the summer between Memorial Day and Labor Day).

ENTRY FEE: $5 per car weekdays, $7 per car weekends (only between Memorial Day and Labor Day). A New Jersey State Park Pass costs $35.00

and is good for a year. It gives you unlimited access to any of the state parks (Cheesequake, Allaire, Round Valley, Sandy Hook).

TRAIL CLASSIFICATIONS: The trail is not marked for difficulty. I would consider it an intermediate trail.

TRAIL MAPS: Trail maps are available at the ranger station by the toll booth.

RESTROOMS: There are seasonal restrooms in the ranger station by the toll booth.

NEARBY MOUNTAIN BIKING AREAS: The Henry Hudson Trail is about five miles east of Cheesequake. Hartshorne Woods Park is about fifteen miles east.

OTHER PARK ACTIVITIES: Hiking, picnicking, camping, softball, fishing and swimming in the Hooks Creek Lake are all popular at Cheesequake. Also, sledding, ice skating, and cross- country skiing are popular during the winter months.

OVERVIEW
The trails at Cheesequake contain some great terrain for mountain biking. Unfortunately, the great majority is off limits to mountain bikes. There are a lot of interesting sites and activities at Cheesequake, which is geared heavily towards education and family fun. Mountain biking is an afterthought at best.

TERRAIN/TRAIL COMPOSITION: The terrain at Cheesequake is relatively technical. The trails are almost entirely singletrack, connected with paved roads. There are many log pile crossings on the singletrack sections, mostly ridable. The terrain is very roller-coaster-esque and challenging. There is some great riding at Cheesequake. Unfortunately, the majority of the park is only accessible on foot.

HISTORY: Cheesequake officially opened in June of 1940. The earliest known inhabitants of the area were the Lenni Lenape Indians. Evidence of their existence dates back some 5000 years.

SPECIFIC TRAIL DIRECTIONS:
Intermediate Loop: The described route is the only trail at Cheesequake where it is legal to ride a mountain bike. There are many miles of other trails at Cheesequake, but bikes are off-limits on all of them. Out of about 15 to 20 trail miles, this three-and-a-half-mile loop encompasses all of the ridable sections of the park.

The route is marked with white circle signs. There are several points where sections of the loop come pretty close to one another, so be careful not to get on an incorrect trail section.

Total route distance: 3.60 miles
Ride time for an intermediate rider: 0.5-1.0 hours

Pt.-Pt.	Cume	Turn	Landmark
0.00	0.00	**L**	Onto paved road. Take it down to end
0.21	0.21	**R**	At stop sign
0.11	0.32	**R**	At next intersection. Go around gate
0.14	0.46	**SL**	Onto beginning of **Multi Use Trail** singletrack
0.37	0.83	**L**	Onto paved road
0.09	0.92	**L**	Onto singletrack Multi Use Trail
0.18	1.10		Short, steep climb
0.22	1.32		Longer, milder climb
0.07	1.39	**BR**	Just before clearing. Follow **white cirle signs**
0.03	1.42	**L**	Onto paved road. Pass the Do Not Enter sign. Road becomes gravel
0.18	1.60	**L**	Onto singletrack trail
0.14	1.74	**L**	Onto gravel road
0.04	1.78	**L**	Onto singletrack trail, bear left immediately
0.18	1.96	**BL**	To continue on white arrow trail
0.05	2.01	**R**	Onto gravel road again
0.04	2.05	**BL**	Onto singletrack trail. Short technical climb
0.07	2.12	**S**	At intersection. Stay on singletrack
0.03	2.15		**Technical stream crossing.** Trail runs along a ridge above a stream
0.22	2.37		Another stream crossing followed directly by a **steep uphill**
0.19	2.56		Top of *technical downhill*
0.04	2.60	**L**	Onto paved road

Pt.-Pt.	Cume	Turn	Landmark
0.01	2.61	**L**	Immediately back onto singletrack
0.05	2.66		Steep climb turning into long extended climb
0.18	2.84	**BR**	Onto paved road. *Long fast downhill*
0.11	2.95	**L**	Watch out for turn before the bottom of the hill! Turn left onto singletrack trail
0.20	3.15		**Short, technical climb**
0.18	3.33	**R**	Onto paved road
0.13	3.46	**L**	At T intersection
0.11	3.57	**L**	At intersection
0.03	3.60		Back to parking lot. End of route

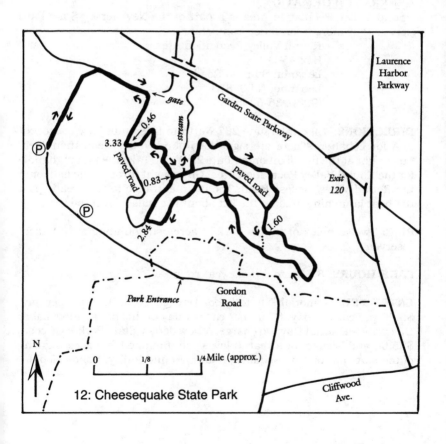

12: Cheesequake State Park

Round Valley Recreation Area—14.74 miles
Lebanon, Hunterdon Co.

HIGHLIGHTS ■ - ◆◆

TERRAIN: Smooth in spots, extremely rocky in
                       others
TOPOGRAPHY: Many steep, extended hills
DIFFICULTY: Moderate to extremely difficult
TRAIL TYPES: Mainly singletrack, limited fire road

GENERAL INFORMATION
Round Valley Recreation Area is a part of the New Jersey State Park
Service. For more information contact:

> Round Valley Recreation Area
> Box 45-D
> Lebanon Stanton Road
> Lebanon, NJ 08833
> (908) 236-6355

DIRECTIONS: Take Interstate 287 North to Interstate 78 West to exit
20A for Lebanon. There are signs for Round Valley Recreation Area.
Turn right at the first light onto Route 22 West. Take the first jughandle
for the Round Valley Recreation Area. Go straight through the light onto
the Round Valley Access Road. The main entrance to the area is past
the boat launching area on the left about two miles down the road.

SIZE: Twelve miles of trails on 1288 acres surrounding a 4003-acre
reservoir.

PARK HOURS: 8 a.m. to 6 p.m., year round.

ENTRY FEE: Memorial Day to Labor Day: $1.00 walk-in fee per day,
$5.00 per car per day, $7.00 per car per day on holidays. After Labor
Day until Memorial Day: no charge. A New Jersey State Park Pass costs
$35.00 and is good for a year. It gives you unlimited free access to any
of the state parks (Cheesequake, Allaire, Round Valley, Sandy Hook).

TRAIL CLASSIFICATIONS: There is one main trail for mountain biking at Round Valley with various spurs and off-shooting loops. The main trail is a nine-mile-long spur starting and finishing near the park entrance and encircling about 75% of the reservoir. The trail is marked with a horseshoe and yellow circles in places, at least for the first three miles or so. I consider the trail to be advanced, with extremely difficult areas.

TRAIL MAPS: Information on many of the state parks is available at the toll booth at the entrance to the park. Trail maps are available there as well.

RESTROOMS: There are restrooms at the toll booth and at various locations around the beach complex. There are also numerous restrooms along the campsite carriage road on the far side of the reservoir.

CLOSEST MOUNTAIN BIKING AREA: Round Valley is fairly isolated. Sourlands Mountain Reserve is about ten to fifteen miles directly southeast.

OTHER PARK ACTIVITIES: Boating, scuba diving, fishing, hunting, swimming, hiking and wilderness camping.

OVERVIEW

Round Valley is the closest of the big-hill, rocky-terrain mountain bike areas to most of Central Jersey. In comparison to Hartshorne, Allaire or Cheesequake, it is an aberration both in terms of its rocky nature and the length and intensity of its climbs. Round Valley is not as close as White Rock or Sourlands, which both are relatively hilly and rocky, but Round Valley is much more of a destination site than anywhere else in the region. After Hartshorne and South Mountain (when it was open), Round Valley is one of the most popular mountain biking areas in the state.

TERRAIN/TRAIL COMPOSITION: The terrain at Round Valley is very large in scale. The hills are much bigger, and the climbs last much longer than at any of the other parks in the area. The nature of the trail as a long spur gives Round Valley the feel of an epic journey in comparison to say, Hartshorne, which would get swallowed up five times in

Round Valley's reservoir alone.

The terrain is rocky overall. In general, it gets progressively more rocky as you head out on the trail. The first three miles are fairly smooth. Once you get into the dense woods on the far side of the reservoir, however, there are numerous sections of extremely rocky terrain, several of which are hard to navigate on foot, let alone on a bike.

HISTORY: Round Valley Recreation Area was opened in the spring of 1977 as a direct result of the 1958 Water Supply Law and the Water Bond Act. Round Valley Reservoir was constructed for the purpose of conserving and effectively managing the water supply. The reservoir is the deepest man-made or natural lake in New Jersey at over 180 feet deep. Before its formation, there was a town in the valley which is now submerged under 55 billion gallons of water.

SPECIFIC TRAIL DIRECTIONS:
Advanced to Abusive Loop: There is only one main trail at Round Valley. The fortunate aspect of the trail (to anyone who feels they have gotten in over their head) is that it is a spur. It is an eighteen-mile ride if you follow it out to the very end and take the same trail back to the start/finish. You can always turn around at any point if you feel you cannot ride the entire length. Also, if you get more than three miles away from the start, you have the option of riding either the singletrack trail up on the higher ground further away from the reservoir or the fire road nearer the reservoir by the campsites. The route will follow the singletrack up on the higher ground on the way out and then return along the fire road.

Total route distance: 14.74 miles
Ride time for an advanced rider: 2.5-4.0 hours

Pt.-Pt.	Cume	Turn	Landmark
0.00	0.00	S	From the **South Parking Lot** take the trail that starts up the grass hill from the parking lot
0.07	0.07	L	Get on the **yellow horseshoe trail** and climb to the top of the hill by the **toll booth**
0.09	0.16	L	Onto singletrack downhill. Trail levels out and becomes roller-coaster-esque

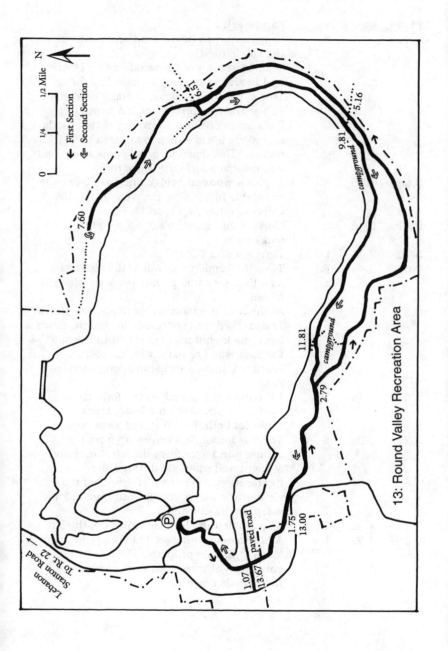

13: Round Valley Recreation Area

Pt.-Pt.	Cume	Turn	Landmark
0.91	1.07	**S**	Cross a narrow paved road and continue on the singletrack
			Trail comes out of the woods into a clearing and **bears right** along a chain link fence. This is the top of a long, sketchy downhill. Follow the trail **left** through a break in the fence and continue down, out of the woods and along a wide-open grass area to the bottom. *This downhill is long and steep, and characterized by lots of loose rocks*
0.68	1.75	**S**	Across a **wooden bridge** and up a basically unridable hill. Follow the trail for awhile. Cross another thin road
0.41	2.16	**S**	Cross a thin gravel road. Stay on the singletrack
0.22	2.38	**L**	Turn left at a T stop
0.06	2.44	**R**	Take the singletrack trail to the **right** at a sign that says it is private property straight ahead
0.35	2.79		At the next intersection there are two paths. The marked trail continues to the left, down a loose, rocky hill that takes you to the start of the campsite fire road, with campsites scattered along a three-mile-long carriage road
0.00	2.79	**R**	Take the right branch at the fork. It continues upwards on a **long, steep, technical climb** with lots of loose rocks
0.27	3.06	**S**	There is a trail that comes up from the campground area from the left. Continue straight and upwards through the intersection. After the trail levels off the singletrack will be rolling with several long, steep, rocky downhills
1.76	4.82	**S**	As a singletrack trail feeds in from the left
0.10	4.92	**L**	At a three-way intersection. The right branch leads to private property. The left branch goes straight through a **rock garden** and then heads downhill

Pt.-Pt.	Cume	Turn	Landmark
0.24	5.16	**S**	Across a gravel road. If you turn left, you will come to the campground carriage road in about 100 yards
0.08	5.24		Begin a **steep, rocky, technical, granny gear climb**
0.35	5.59		Top of a _long, fast, rocky downhill_
0.23	5.82	**R**	When the downhill starts to level off there is a right trail that runs parallel to the shoreline. From this point the trail gets increasingly rocky and technical. There are several **extremely technical rock garden sections**
0.16	5.98		**Short, rocky, technical, granny gear climb**
0.53	6.51	**S**	Across wider trail which leads down to the end of the campsite carriage road
			The overall shape of the route is a loop with a spur off each end of it. This point is the far end of the loop. From here, the route continues out as a spur along increasingly technical singletrack up to the top of a very large hill and then back to this point. Once you return to this point, the route will continue on the loop, which is this left turn
0.91	7.42	**S**	After **numerous rock gardens** along a relatively level singletrack, you will get to a **very long, steep, unridable hill**
0.18	7.60		At the top of the hill there is a four-way intersection. This is the end of the spur portion of the route. Continuing straight will take you out to a series of paved roads that you can take the rest of the way around to the parking lot in four to five miles
			Turn around and head back down the hill. This is an **_extremely technically difficult, dangerous downhill_**. If you are not a **very** strong technical rider, I suggest turning around at the bottom of the hill before you climb to the top
1.10	8.70	**R**	Back to the four-way intersection (6.51 miles). Turn right onto the short trail

Pt.-Pt.	Cume	Turn	Landmark
			downhill to the **campsite carriage road**
0.05	8.75	**L**	Onto the **carriage road**, which runs roughly parallel to the shoreline of the reservoir for the next three miles
1.06	9.81	**S**	Take the middle of the three forks
2.00	11.81	**S**	At a four-way intersection. The trail becomes singletrack and climbs up a **loose, rocky, technical hill**
0.13	11.94	**R**	At three-way intersection at the top of the hill
0.35	12.29	**L**	Onto a fire road at a T intersection
0.06	12.35	**R**	Onto a _long, rocky, downhill fire road_
0.22	12.57	**S**	Across a small gravel road
0.35	12.92		Top of a _short, but extremely steep, technical downhill_
0.08	13.00	**S**	Across a paved road at the bottom of the hill. This is the beginning of a **very, very long, grinding, frustrating granny gear climb**
0.27	13.27	**R**	After crossing a chain link fence. Keep climbing. The trail is not quite as steep as the previous section, but there are a lot of loose rocks to contend with
0.40	13.67	**S**	Across a small paved road. Stay on singletrack
0.91	14.58	**R**	At three-way intersection at the top of the hill at the final singletrack downhill
0.09	14.67	**R**	At clearing and continue down to the parking lot
0.07	14.74		Back to parking lot. End of route

Mercer County Park—13.04 miles
Hamilton & West Windsor, Mercer Co.

HIGHLIGHTS ● - ■

TERRAIN: Very rooty in spots, smooth in others, numerous ridable logs and log piles

TOPOGRAPHY: Almost completely flat

DIFFICULTY: Moderate

TRAIL TYPES: Mostly singletrack, some paved connecting trails

GENERAL INFORMATION
Mercer County Park is a part of the Mercer County Parks System. For more information contact:

> Mercer County Parks Commission
> 640 S. Broad St.
> P.O. Box 8068
> Trenton, NJ 08650
> (609) 989-6530

DIRECTIONS: Take Route 1 to Quakerbridge Road south (Route 533). In about two miles, turn left onto Hughes Ave. The park entrance is a half mile on the left. Take the first left off of the park road and park at the West Picnic Area.

SIZE: About 14 miles of trails on 2600 acres.

PARK HOURS: Dawn to dusk, year round.

ENTRY FEE: No charge.

TRAIL CLASSIFICATIONS: There is one main marked trail with several offshoots. It is moderate. There are some extremely rooty sections, but overall, the trail is suitable for most riders.

TRAIL MAPS: No detailed maps of the trail system at Mercer exist. There is one marked, paved bicycle path, and one main trail that circumnavigates the lake with numerous offshoots.

RESTROOMS: There are facilities in the West Picnic Area and by the boat house.

CLOSEST MOUNTAIN BIKING AREA: Sourlands Mountain Preserve is about fifteen miles northwest of Mercer, and Clayton Park is about ten miles east.

OTHER PARK ACTIVITIES: Boating is permitted in the lake from mid-April through October. Gas motors are not permitted. Fishing, hiking and picnicking are popular at Mercer, and there are athletic fields where softball and soccer teams compete. During the winter months there is an ice skating rink and cross-country skiing if the conditions allow.

OVERVIEW
The main trail at Mercer is a long loop (about 10 miles). There are numerous trails which branch off the main trail. Most do not go anywhere. The main trail is not well marked, and it is easy to get lost. I have been riding at Mercer for years, and I still average at least one wrong turn per ride. Mountain biking at Mercer is allowed only by default. The trails are multi-use, and I have never been hassled about riding my bike anywhere at Mercer, but the rangers I have talked to do not seem to be too enamored with mountain bikers in general.

TERRAIN/TRAIL COMPOSITION: Mercer County Park is located on what is probably the flattest parcel of land of any serious mountain biking area in New Jersey. It also probably has the worst drainage. Much of Mercer turns into a swamp whenever it rains and remains so for weeks after any serious rainfall. There is a noticeable lack of rocks at Mercer. Aside from several short sections, rocks are almost nonexistent. The major obstacle to smooth ground at Mercer is roots. Throughout the park there are a plethora of exposed roots, so much so that in sections it is difficult to navigate the trail on foot, let alone on bicycle.

The other major obstacles at Mercer are fallen logs. They are scattered all throughout the singletrack trails, but depending on your riding ability, the vast majority of them are ridable. Most of the larger logs have been built up with sticks and branches to form ramps which are easier to navigate.

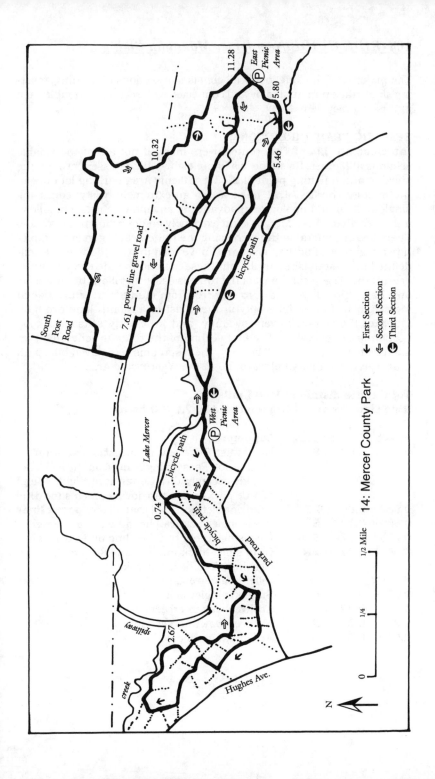

14: Mercer County Park

0   1/4   1/2 Mile

← First Section
⇙ Second Section
◐ Third Section

East Picnic Area

11.28

5.80

5.46

bicycle path

South Post Road

7.61 power line gravel road

10.32

Lake Mercer

West Picnic Area

bicycle path

bicycle path

0.74

park road

2.67

spillway

creek

Hughes Ave.

N

The majority of the long loop trail consists of sections of winding, twisting singletrack punctuated by and connected with sections of doubletrack and paved bicycle path.

SPECIFIC TRAIL DIRECTIONS:

Intermediate Loop: This route covers most, if not all, of the ridable sections at Mercer. Its shape is a figure eight, which passes through the starting and finishing point of the West Picnic Area parking lot once in the middle. The first 4.11 miles are in an extremely twisty, confusing singletrack area. I apologize in advance to anyone who gets lost following these directions. Mercer is an extremely confounding place to ride. There are innumerable trails crossing the route heading in every direction imaginable. For the most part, I have tried to stick to the most well-defined and established trails, but these may not be the same in a few years' time. The second part of the route is easier to follow, but it has its own hardships. If you want to stay free from mud for an entire ride at Mercer, plan to ride here only in the midst of a month-long drought. Much of the terrain is very swampy, and in a rainy season, a good portion is under water. The first section of the route is generally drier and twistier. The route will begin by the rest rooms on a paved bike path that passes by a small playground in the West Picnic Area.

Total route distance: 13.04 miles
Ride time for an intermediate rider: 2.0-3.0 hours

PtPt.	Cume	Turn	Landmark
0.00	0.00	**S**	Head west. Take paved path **straight** out from parking lot. Pass a **playground** on the left. Trail quickly becomes dirt. Continue straight. At end of little park area, drop down eroded sandy hill
0.06	0.06	**L**	Onto doubletrack road that follows **power lines**
0.06	0.12	**S**	Pass singletrack trail heading off to the right
0.05	0.17	**S**	Pass singletrack trail heading off to the right
0.04	0.21	**BR**	Onto singletrack into woods after small clearing. Trail becomes rolling and roller-coaster-esque
0.07	0.28	**L**	Stay on singletrack
0.04	0.32	**R**	At three-way intersection
0.01	0.33	**R**	At three-way intersection
0.04	0.37	**R**	At four-way intersection

Pt.-Pt.	Cume	Turn	Landmark
0.02	0.39	L	Down and up across old dirt road. Stay on singletrack
0.05	0.44	R	At BMX-type jump area with numerous jumps
0.02	0.46	S	At end of jump area back onto singletrack
0.06	0.52	L	At three-way intersection
0.22	0.74	L/R	Come out onto paved bike route. Make a **left** and an immediate **right** back onto singletrack on the other side
0.22	0.96	R	Take the **right** fork on the low path along the banks of **Lake Mercer**
0.06	1.02	L	At three-way intersection. Come out into clearing
0.04	1.06	S	Across built-up dam embankment trail. Stay on singletrack
0.06	1.12	R	At four-way intersection. Singletrack trail heads into woods
0.01	1.13	S	Pass a right turn
0.10	1.23	L	At three-way intersection. This section is extremely twisty as it navigates a **dense young forest area**
0.06	1.29	L	At three-way intersection
0.01	1.30	S	At multiple intersection
0.02	1.32	R	At three-way intersection. Trail enters a more spread-out, **older growth area**
0.08	1.40	L	At three-way intersection
0.02	1.42	L	At three-way intersection. Stay in the woods
0.04	1.46	S	At four-way intersection. Singletrack trail runs along the border of a clearing
0.16	1.62	R	At three-way intersection onto twisty singletrack
0.06	1.68	L	At three-way intersection around a fallen tree
0.02	1.70	R	At four-way intersection onto straight singletrack
0.02	1.72	L	At T intersection onto a more well defined singletrack trail. Stay on this well defined trail past numerous cutoffs and side trails
0.12	1.84	S	Across a creek crossing built up with logs
0.05	1.89	R	At three-way intersection
0.07	1.96	BR	As trail comes in from the left
0.10	2.06	R	At three-way intersection. Come out into a

Pt.-Pt.	Cume	Turn	Landmark
			clearing. Pass the remnants of a shooting range. Trail becomes singletrack again
0.11	2.17	**R**	At three-way intersection as trail comes in from the left. This section of trail runs alongside the creek that flows from **Lake Mercer**
0.07	2.24	**L**	Down and up across small stream. Stay on the closest trail to the water in this whole section
0.43	2.67	**R**	Come out into the clearing by the **spillway** and stay along treeline
0.03	2.70	**R**	Back into woods. Stay on singletrack
0.03	2.73	**L**	At three-way intersection. This section is very sandy
0.04	2.77	**S**	At four-way intersection. Trail heads into more densely wooded area
0.01	2.78	**L**	Take **left** fork into woods
0.03	2.81	**L**	Stay along the perimeter of the clearing
0.02	2.83	**R**	Stay on twisty singletrack trail
0.08	2.91	**L**	At three-way intersection. Go straight through the next few small intersections
0.03	2.94	**R**	At three-way intersection. Stay in the woods
0.07	3.01	**R**	At three-way intersection into older growth, less dense woods
0.10	3.11	**L**	Into clearing on wider, more defined trail
0.07	3.18	**S**	Cross built-up dam road
0.03	3.21		Enter woods by the banks of the lake
0.27	3.48	**L/R**	Re-cross paved bike path
0.22	3.70	**L**	At T intersection
0.04	3.74	**S**	Down and up across old dirt road. Stay on singletrack
0.04	3.78	**L**	At three-way intersection
0.01	3.79	**R**	Stay **right** at three-way intersection
0.04	3.83	**BR**	Through a few intersections. This section is roller-coaster-esque
0.06	3.89	**L**	Onto power-line doubletrack trail
0.14	4.03	**R**	Climb up short sandy hill. Pass playground
0.08	4.11		Back to parking lot. End of first section of route

Second part of route:

Pt.-Pt.	Cume	Turn	Landmark
	4.11		Head out in the opposite direction to the end of the parking lot toward an arched wooden footbridge. Get onto **paved bike path**
0.11	4.22	**S**	Across **wooden footbridge**
0.09	4.31	**BL**	Onto dirt path along edge of lake
0.07	4.38	**S**	Across a paved road and continue straight. Stay near the edge of the lake heading towards the woods
0.07	4.45	**S**	Cross another paved road and get onto a dirt path
0.08	4.53	**S**	Enter woods. Trail narrows down to singletrack
0.12	4.65	**S**	Come out into clearing. Head straight across. Follow sandy singletrack along edge of lake
0.07	4.72	**S**	Re-enter woods
0.21	4.93	**S**	Pass a right turn. Stay along edge of lake
0.14	5.07	**BR**	Trail heads up steep hill away from the lake
0.02	5.09	**L**	Head back down a steep hill towards the lake
0.03	5.12	**S**	Pass a right turn
0.05	5.17	**S**	Trail comes out into a clearing by the **tennis center** and runs along the treeline
0.06	5.23	**L**	Trail heads back into the woods. This section is very rooty
0.12	5.35	**BL**	Trail comes out into clearing and immediately goes back into the woods to the left
0.11	5.46	**L**	Onto a **paved bike path**
0.34	5.80	**S**	Across an **arched wooden footbridge**. Stay on paved path
0.10	5.90	**S**	Enter a parking lot
0.04	5.94	**L**	By the restroom building
0.02	5.96	**S**	Take singletrack into woods
0.08	6.04	**L**	Onto wider, straight trail
0.20	6.24	**S**	At four-way intersection
0.05	6.29	**S**	Across an unridable creek crossing. The first part of the crossing seems to have been washed away, and it is hard to navigate on foot
0.01	6.30	**L**	At three-way intersection on other side of bridge
0.29	6.59	**S**	Quick down and up across a stream bed
0.32	6.91	**L**	At three-way intersection onto wider trail

PtPt.	Cume	Turn	Landmark
0.02	6.93	**S**	Across a creek
0.01	6.94	**R**	Onto thin singletrack. This section is very twisty. Throughout this section stay on the main trail. Pass numerous spurs
0.58	7.52	**R**	At four-way intersection towards clearing
0.04	7.56	**R**	At clearing. Trail runs along treeline perimeter
0.05	7.61	**L**	Onto **powerline gravel road**
0.25	7.86	**R**	Onto paved road after passing through a gravel parking lot
0.08	7.94	**R**	Onto doubletrack heading into woods
0.07	8.01	**L**	By pond. Trail narrows down into singletrack. Cross several **stick bridges** through muddy sections
0.10	8.11	**S**	Trail comes out into clearing and heads right back into woods along treeline
0.30	8.41	**S**	Trail comes out into clearing, heads back in, comes out and heads back into woods
0.05	8.46	**S**	Across a stream crossing on a plank
0.09	8.55	**S**	Cross a small stream on a plank
0.06	8.61	**S**	Across a stream on a plank. The singletrack trail becomes twisty
0.21	8.82	**S**	Climb a short hill. This section of trail (almost to the end of the route) is marked with **fluorescent orange paint blazes**
0.77	9.59	**S**	Cross a stream. Stay on the singletrack
0.06	9.65	**S**	At four-way intersection across a doubletrack road
0.07	9.72	**S**	Trail comes out onto a **farm field**. Trail runs along the perimeter of the field
0.12	9.84	**L**	Singletrack heads back into the woods
0.08	9.92	**S**	Into woods. Cross a swampy section and climb up onto a small plateau
0.05	9.97	**R**	At top of plateau
0.07	10.04	**S**	Cross a plank over a stream. This section is hilly and roller-coaster-esque
0.13	10.17	**R**	Get off roller coaster onto flat ground
0.13	10.30	**S**	Trail comes out into clearing at **power lines**
0.02	10.32	**L**	Onto **gravel doubletrack road** following powerline

Pt.-Pt.	Cume	Turn	Landmark
0.08	10.40	**R**	Onto singletrack into the woods. This section is **very muddy and rooty**
0.09	10.49	**R**	At T intersection. Pass a drainage pipe on the left
0.03	10.52	**S**	Cross a stream. This is a **very swampy section**
0.08	10.60	**S**	Trail gets back onto drier ground
0.02	10.62	**R**	At three-way intersection. Follow fluorescent orange blazes
0.36	10.98	**L**	At four-way intersection onto wider singletrack trail
0.23	11.21	**S**	Onto paved road
0.07	11.28	**R**	Onto paved road. Pass through gravel parking lot. Head for **paved bike path** at far right corner of parking lot
0.18	11.46	**S**	Re-cross an **arched wooden footbridge**
0.72	12.18	**S**	Cross two paved bike paths
0.05	12.23	**BR**	Stay on paved bike path
0.41	12.64	**S**	Onto dirt path as paved path turns left
0.09	12.73	**S**	Cross a paved road. Climb up to a parking lot
0.09	12.82	**BR**	Get back onto paved bike path
0.05	12.87	**R**	At three-way intersection. Stay on paved path
0.09	12.96	**S**	Re-cross an **arched wooden footbridge**
0.08	13.04		Back to parking lot. End of route

Ringwood State Park—6.57/8.63 miles
Ringwood, Passaic Co.

HIGHLIGHTS   ■ - ◆

TERRAIN:	Extremely rocky in sections, fairly rocky everywhere
TOPOGRAPHY:	Very hilly, almost mountainous. Lots of long, extended climbs
DIFFICULTY:	Intermediate to technically and aerobically advanced
TRAIL TYPES:	Lots of technical fire road, innumerable singletrack trails

GENERAL INFORMATION

Ringwood State Park is a part of the New Jersey Division of Parks and Forestry. For more information contact:

Ringwood State Park
Box 1304
Ringwood, NJ 07456
(973) 962-7031

DIRECTIONS: Take Route 17 north to Interstate 287 north into New York State. Take the first exit for Route 17 north and stay on the road for about two miles. Take the jughandle for Sloatsburg Road and continue for four miles. Turn left into the park at the Skylands/Shepherd Lake entrance and take the road to the top of the hill. Turn left at the stop sign and follow it to the Shepherd Lake toll booth. Park in the parking lot up to the left.

SIZE: More than thirty miles of trails on 4054 acres.

PARK HOURS: Dawn to dusk, year round.

ENTRY FEE: Fees are charged during the peak season for parking at the Shepherd Lake, Ringwood and Skylands sections of the park. The New Jersey State Park Pass costs $35.00 and is good for a year. It gives you unlimited access to any of the state parks (Cheesequake, Allaire,

Round Valley, Sandy Hook).

TRAIL CLASSIFICATIONS: None of the trails at Ringwood are marked for difficulty. There are seven color-coded, marked trails.

TRAIL MAPS: Trail maps can be obtained at the bath house at Shepherd Lake

RESTROOMS: Restrooms are located in the bath house at Shepherd Lake.

NEARBY MOUNTAIN BIKING AREAS: Wawayanda State Park is about 10-15 miles west of the western end of Ringwood.

OTHER PARK ACTIVITIES: Hiking, swimming, boating, hunting, shooting, fishing, picnicking, cross-country skiing and snowmobiling are all popular activities at Ringwood.

OVERVIEW
Ringwood is a large state park that contains countless miles of great off-road riding. The park is situated on more than four thousand acres of land, and there are trails running over it in every conceivable direction. The park is bordered to the south by Ramapo State Forest.

Beyond the sheer size of Ringwood, there is also an element of vastness that you do not find at most of the mountain biking areas in New Jersey. As opposed to Hartshorne, Mercer, or Lewis Morris, Ringwood is not surrounded on all sides by suburban sprawl. Virtually none of the borders of the park are roads, or even backstreets. I've gotten lost in Ringwood and was unable to find a paved road until I was five to ten miles outside the park boundary by Interstate 287. Ringwood is the closest thing to wilderness that New Jersey offers.

TERRAIN/TRAIL COMPOSITION: If you come from the southern part of the state, the first thing you will notice when you begin to ride Ringwood is that it is rocky. Compared to most of the parks in Central Jersey, Ringwood is full of rocky terrain and littered with rock gardens. The next thing you will notice is that the climbs do not level off after a short time, but continue upwards for miles. Ringwood is part of the same range of mountains which cover the northwestern region

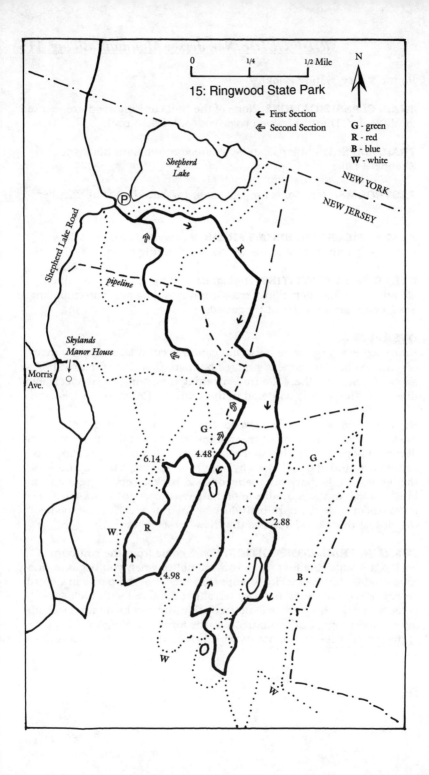

of the state and make alpine skiing possible in New Jersey.

Ringwood is divided by a rocky pipeline fire road and is riddled with numerous other fire roads, which crisscross each other throughout the park. In general, these are rocky and not navigable by anything other than serious four-wheel-drives and quads, which you will encounter occassionally. From these relatively stable thoroughfares emanate a whole slew of singletrack trails that twist and turn their way throughout the park.

HISTORY: Ringwood became the property of Abram S. Hewitt in the mid-1800s Century after producing many essential items for the colonies during the American Revolution. In 1936, the original property of the Ringwood Manor House and its surrounding 95 acres were deeded to the State of New Jersey. Since then the state has added much of the remaining acreage to the park under the Green Acres program, including the 1966 acquisition of the Skylands Manor estate.

Skylands Manor, built by Clarence MacKenzie Lewis in the 1920s as a summer house, has been maintained as a fine example of an English Jacobean mansion. Ringwood Manor House remains an accurate depiction of Hewitt's life in the late nineteenth and early twentieth centuries. It is a National Historic Landmark.

SPECIFIC TRAIL DIRECTIONS:
Advanced Loop: This route combines fire road and technical multi-track riding with a lot of spectacular singletrack. Ringwood is a very hilly, almost mountainous area. The trails are very strenuous. This route includes most of the highlights of the park.

Total route distance: 6.57/8.63 miles
Ride guide for advanced rider: 1.5-2.5 hours

Pt.-Pt.	Cume	Turn	Landmark
0.0	0.0	**S**	This route starts at the parking lot just inside the **Shepherd's Lake** gate and to the right by the boathouse. Get on the **red trail** fire road and head straight
0.70	0.70	**BR**	Climb up hill at intersection heading away from the end of the lake

Pt.-Pt.	Cume	Turn	Landmark
0.13	0.83	**S**	At intersection after the trail levels out. Trail becomes singletrack
0.58	1.41	**SL**	Switchback turn near bottom of *steep downhill*
0.07	1.48	**R**	The trail levels out
0.13	1.61	**R**	Stay to the right and head up **loose-rocky climb.** The first part of the climb is very steep, but then becomes a longer, more gradual climb
0.10	1.71	**R**	Onto singletrack climb which then levels out and becomes multitrack
0.09	1.80	**S**	**Short, rocky climb**
0.20	2.00	**S**	Becomes singletrack again
0.10	2.10	**S**	**Really rocky, technical section**
0.08	2.18	**S**	At intersection. Cross wider trail. Stay on singletrack
0.04	2.22	**S**	Rocky, technical, serpentine gradual climb
0.15	2.37	**S**	At intersection. Cross wide-open **pipeline road.** Stay on singletrack
0.07	2.44	**BR**	Onto wider fire road
0.07	2.51	**BL**	Take the left fork that heads up long, gradual fire road climb
0.37	2.88	**L**	At three-way intersection
0.05	2.93	**R**	At three-way intersection. Trail is still fire road and becomes **fast downhill**
0.35	3.28	**L**	**Bear left** and take **immediate left** onto singletrack. Windy singletrack trail runs roughly parallel to fire road
0.19	3.47	**S**	Cross fire road. Stay on singletrack. Trail becomes *twisty, technical downhill* with a switchback turn. Stay on singletrack
0.09	3.56	**S**	Trail gradually begins long climb
0.09	3.65	**L**	At top of hill onto level fire road. Quickly becomes *long, fast downhill*
0.39	4.04	**S**	At intersection. *Watch out for water channels*
0.44	4.48	**L**	**If** you want to do about a 6.5-mile loop turn **right** here and skip down to the second half of the loop. Otherwise, **turn left** onto **white/ green dot trail** here for an extra two miles of

Pt.-Pt.	Cume	Turn	Landmark
			spectacular singletrack riding
0.50	4.98	**R**	Onto steep doubletrack trail. This is the start of a **long grinding climb**
0.15	5.13	**R**	Onto wider doubletrack trail. Continue to climb
0.07	5.20	**R**	At intersection at top of hill onto **Red Trail**. Trail remains doubletrack and continues to climb
0.58	5.78	**R**	Onto **Red Trail** singletrack. Rocky, technical climb
0.29	6.07	**S**	Top of hill. There is a left spur that climbs up about twenty yards to a beautiful overlook. It is a good break after a long climb. Beautiful view of **Ringwood Manor House, Wanaque Reservoir** and miles of Northern New Jersey mountains
0.07	6.14	**R**	At three-way intersection onto **White/Green Dot Trail**. This is the top of *an intensely technical downhill.* There are **sixteen switchback turns** to the valley floor. This is an easy place to break a collarbone
0.40	6.54	**L**	Back onto fire road

Second Half of Loop:

Pt.-Pt.	Cume	Turn	Landmark
0.02	6.56	**S**	After a 2.06-mile loop we are back to the original route. If you didn't turn left way back at mile 4.49, make a right onto fire road. This is the **White/Green Dot Trail**
0.15	6.71	**L**	Take the **left fork** after passing through the gate of a **nineteenth century stone manor**
0.16	6.87	**L**	Onto **long, steep granny gear climb.** Most people don't stay on their bikes too long
0.14	7.01	**S**	Top of hill. Trail becomes singletrack
0.10	7.11	**S**	At intersection across pipeline road. Stay on singletrack
0.17	7.28	**S**	At intersection across wider trail. Stay on singletrack

Pt.-Pt.	Cume	Turn	Landmark
0.57	7.85	**S**	At intersection across thin doubletrack. Stay on singletrack
0.08	7.93	**SR**	Stay on trail as it twists around to the right
0.54	8.47	**L**	Onto original boathouse fire road. Lake will be to your right
0.16	8.63		Back to parking lot. End of route

Allamuchy Mountain Park—7.90 miles
Hackettstown, Warren, Sussex & Morris Co.

HIGHLIGHTS   ■ - ◆◆

TERRAIN: Somewhat smooth in parts,
                     extremely rocky in others
TOPOGRAPHY: Many long, extended hills
DIFFICULTY: Intermediate to extremely difficult
TRAIL TYPES: Mostly singletrack, some fire road
                     sections

GENERAL INFORMATION
Allamuchy Mountain Park is a part of the New Jersey State Park Service. For more information contact:

> Allamuchy Mountain & Stephens State Parks
> 800 Willow Grove Street
> Hackettstown, NJ 07840
> (908) 852-3790

DIRECTIONS: *To Allamuchy Natural Area:* Take I-80 to the Hackettstown/Andover exit 19 for Rt. 517. Turn left at the end of the exit ramp onto Rt. 517 South. Turn left onto a dirt road, Deer Park Road, after 2.3 miles. Follow the very rocky, rutted-out dirt road for 0.7 miles and park at the first parking lot. The trailhead for the route is off to the left.

To the Northeastern Section: Take I-80 to the exit for Rt. 206 north. Take the first jughandle for International Drive. Turn right at the first intersection. Take this road for half a mile to a T intersection for Waterloo Rd. The parking lot is straight across the intersection. The trailhead is at the far end of the small parking lot.

SIZE: More than 15 miles of trails in the Allamuchy Natural Area Section. Many more than 20 miles of trails in the Northern Section.

PARK HOURS: Dawn to dusk, year round.

ENTRY FEE: No charge.

TRAIL CLASSIFICATIONS: None of the trails at Allamuchy are marked for difficulty. The trails in the Natural Area are well marked Yellow, White, Red or Blue. Several of the trails in the Northern Section are poorly marked, and many more are not marked at all.

TRAIL MAPS: Trail maps are periodically available at the first parking lot in the Natural Area at the information board. Trail maps are always available at the park office in the Stephens State Park Section.

RESTROOMS: There is a restroom at the first parking lot in the Allamuchy Natural Area. Restrooms are also located at several places in the Stephens Section.

NEARBY MOUNTAIN BIKING AREAS: Mahlon Dickerson is about 15-20 miles east.

OTHER PARK ACTIVITIES: Hiking, camping, picnicking, fishing, hunting, cross-country skiing, snowshoeing and sightseeing.

OVERVIEW
Allamuchy is a large park (9200 acres) made up of three distinct sections that correspond almost perfectly with the three counties that divide the park. Stephens State Park is the southernmost section, and it is located in Morris County. All of the campgrounds at Allamuchy are located in this section, which straddles the Musconetcong River.

The Allamuchy Natural Area is northwest of Stephens. It is entirely in Warren County. There are several extremely steep trail spurs leading up from Waterloo Rd. by the river, but otherwise the entire trail system of the natural area is high atop the ridge overlooking the Musconetcong River.

The remaining section makes up about half of the entire acreage of Allamuchy. It is almost entirely in Sussex County, but small sections are in Warren and Morris Counties as well. The trail system in this section is not very well marked, and it is a wild, rocky, overgrown place. Cranberry Lake and Jefferson Lake are both in this section.

Waterloo village is separated from the rest of this section by Waterloo

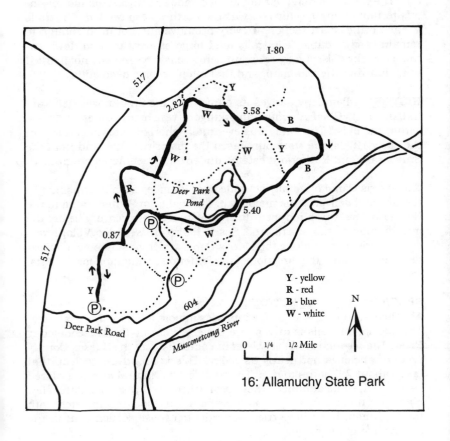

I-80

517

2.82

W

3.58

B

Y

W

W

Y

B

R

Deer Park
Pond

5.40

0.87

P

W

P

Y

517

P

Deer Park Road

604

Musconetcong River

Y - yellow
R - red
B - blue
W - white

N

0   1/4   1/2 Mile

16: Allamuchy State Park

124 RIDE GUIDE/New Jersey Mountain Biking

Road to the north. Waterloo Village contains a replica of a 400-year-old Delaware Indian Village as well as the remains of an old port village along the now-defunct Morris Canal.

TERRAIN/TRAIL COMPOSITION: The trails at Allamuchy are very diverse. The Natural Area trail system is well marked and well thought out. The terrain is hilly, but not as well endowed with steep mountainous terrain or as ruggedly rocky as the northeastern section. The trails in the northeastern section are very primitive and not used enough to remain easily ridable. The trails tend to go straight up and down extremely rocky hills, and there are numerous offshoots that are not marked or included in the trail map, and that often become dead ends.

HISTORY: Allamuchy derives its name from the first known Delaware Indian chief, Chief Allamuchahokkingen, which translates to "place within the hills." The name was eventually shortened to Allamuchy. In the early 1970s, the state purchased the majority of the land from the Stuyvesant and Rutherford estates under the Green Acres program.

The Morris Canal originally stretched ninety miles from Phillipsburg to Newark and delivered the majority of the coal from Pennsylvania to the Northern Jersey iron industry during the nineteenth century before the introduction of the Morris and Essex Railroad. Waterloo Village was once a thriving port along the Morris Canal which has become a tourist destination under the direction of the Waterloo Foundation for the Arts, Inc.

SPECIFIC TRAIL DIRECTIONS:
Advanced Loop: This loop encompasses almost all of the Natural Area. This section of trails is high above the gorge cut by the Musconetcong River. The terrain is relatively level in comparison to the Sussex County section, and it is not nearly as rocky. This is an advanced loop that takes about 2.5 hours to ride. The trails in the Natural Area are blazed yellow, red, white and blue. They are marked fairly well. There are a few places on this route which do not seem to correspond completely with the trail map, but I have tried to straighten those sections out in the description of the route.

Total route distance: 7.90 miles
Ride time for an advanced rider: 2.0-3.0 hours

Pt.-Pt.	Cume	Turn	Landmark
0.0	0.0		Ride away from the information board at the first parking lot, across the clearing and onto the **Yellow Trail** which starts by crossing a **small dam**
0.04	0.04	**S**	Enter **Yellow Trail** trailhead. After crossing the dam, the singletrack trail begins a **long, grinding climb**
0.66	0.70		Trail levels off up top after 220 vertical feet and descends to first intersection
0.17	0.87	**L**	At three-way intersection onto the **Red Trail**
0.43	1.30		Stream crossing at the bottom of a downhill
0.20	1.50	**L**	Onto **White Trail** at three-way intersection
0.33	1.83	**S**	Pass a right turn in the middle of a climb
0.99	2.82	**S**	Pass a left turn, which leads out to a scenic overlook that is a rest area for eastbound **Interstate 80** travelers
0.23	3.05	**R**	After climbing a total of 100 vertical feet in this last section, turn right at three-way intersection. Stay on **White Trail**
0.34	3.39		Top of *long downhill*. Fallen tree obstructing trail about four feet off the ground. You can ride up and around it to the left. There is another high fallen tree nearly at the bottom of the downhill
0.19	3.58	**L**	At a fork onto the **Blue Trail**, which isn't marked for awhile
0.65	4.23	**BR**	At fork. Stay on **Blue Trail**
0.09	4.32		Cross stream
0.28	4.60		Trail begins to twist and climb. The trail crosses back and forth across the remnants of an old stone fence several times
0.19	4.79		Top of *steep technical downhill*
0.04	4.83		Water crossing at the bottom of the downhill. After the water crossing, the trail winds through a **long rock garden** and then climbs up a **long, grinding hill**
0.39	5.22		Top of hill overlooking **Deer Park Pond**. The trail has climbed 280 vertical feet in the last 2.5 miles. Trail heads downhill to pond.

Pt.-Pt.	Cume	Turn	Landmark
0.18	5.40	**L**	At T intersection onto the **White Trail** fire road, which circumnavigates the pond
0.08	5.48	**BR**	Stay on the fire road as it turns right after crossing the concrete spillway. Pass a left turn for a singletrack trail
0.88	6.36	**R**	Get onto singletrack just before a **yellow gate** across the fire road
0.04	6.40	**L**	At three-way intersection onto **Red Trail**
0.20	6.60		Water crossing followed by a **fairly long, steep, technical climb**
0.43	7.03	**R**	At three-way intersection onto **Yellow Trail**
0.35	7.38		Top of *long, steep, rutted, rocky, technical downhill*
0.17	7.55	**BR**	The **Yellow Trail** continues to the right at a powerline intersection. The trail is still going downhill and *gets steeper, rockier and more technical*
0.28	7.83		Re-cross small dam
0.02	7.85		Come out into clearing
0.05	7.90		Back to parking lot. End of route

FAVORITE PLACES TO RIDE OUTSIDE OF NEW JERSEY

There are countless places outside New Jersey that contain incredible riding. Here are a few of my favorite places to ride when I have several free days in a row and some gas in the tank.

Wissahickon Park, Philadelphia, Pennsylvania

Within the city of Philadelphia, Wissahickon Park is the northwest portion of Fairmount Park, which is geographically the largest inner-city park in America. Wissahickon has at least twenty-five miles of spectacular riding. There is a spot atop a ridge at Wissahickon where I always feel as though I have been transported to a high mountain meadow somewhere deep in the Rockies. The trails at Wissahickon are centered around a gravel carriage road that runs alongside the Wissahickon Creek at the bottom of a very steep valley. All the technical trails run parallel to the carriage road on both sides of the valley, but high up along a ridge. There are innumerable trails linking the singletrack with the carriage road, some at a gradual, ridable pace up and some straight up loose, rocky, unridable sections. Once you are up top on one of the singletrack trails, you can stay up there on some exhilarating roller-coaster-esque singletrack that only comes down to the valley floor on a few occasions. You can also exit the ridge-top trails every quarter or half mile and be back down on the carriage road in minutes.

There is a biking fee that was instituted in 1996. For thirty dollars, you are allowed complete access to all the trails for one year. There are several places to enter the park in an auto, but none with facilities to collect the fee. There is presently no penalty for being caught riding without a permit, but you will have to pay the thirty-dollar fee. There is a small building located at the southeastern end of the carriage road where you should be able to find more current information.

DIRECTIONS: Whenever I have been at Wissahickon, I have used the entrance off Henry Ave. for the Valley Green. Drive down the narrow, winding road for about a half mile until it dumps you onto the carriage road. Turn right and park at the parking lot about a quarter mile down the carriage road.

Jim Thorpe, Pennsylvania

Jim Thorpe is a town, not a specific park. It is located about 20 miles northwest of Allentown in the Pocono Mountains. Hundreds and hundreds of miles of trails wind out and away from the town in all directions and include everything from hybrid-friendly trails to routes where dual suspension is a must. Jim Thorpe is very mountain bike friendly. There is a mountain bike festival weekend every June and there are a number of mountain bike touring companies based in town. A mountain bike guide book, which includes 13 rides in the area, can be purchased at Blue Mountain Sports right in town. The employees are very friendly and will gladly give you recommendations for rides based on your ability and the amount of time on your hands.

The town of Jim Thorpe is very scenic and rich in historical landmarks. Reminiscent of Park City, Utah, or Breckenridge, Colorado, the restored Victorian mining town is set in a valley among some steep mountains. Jim Thorpe is also a very popular destination for white water rafting.

DIRECTIONS: From most points in New Jersey the fastest way to get to Jim Thorpe is to take Interstate 78 West into Pennsylvania and just past Allentown to the northeast extension of the Pennsylvania Turnpike (Rt. 9). Take the turnpike north through the Lehigh Tunnel one exit to exit 34. Take U.S. Highway 209 southwest and follow signs for Jim Thorpe.

Plattekill Ski Area, Roxbury, New York

Plattekill is located in the Catskill Mountains of New York. It is about a two-hour drive from the New Jersey border up the New York Thruway (Interstate 87). Plattekill has been a ski resort for decades, and after closing for a few years, was re-opened in 1995 by a young new owner, who is turning it into a mountain bike Mecca during the off season. Plattekill has been host to numerous National Off-Road Bicycle Association (NORBA)-sanctioned races since reopening, including cross-country, downhill, and dual slalom. The lift is opened on weekends and holidays between April and November. A daily lift ticket and trail access is a bargain at $18. Trail access alone without the use of the lift is $10 a day, which is a little steep in comparison. The mountain covers roughly 1000 vertical feet and there is a labyrinth of trails running all over the mountain. The trails are well maintained and run the gauntlet from wide-open fire roads to tricky, technical singletrack. For more information call (800) GOTTA-BIKE.

DIRECTIONS: To get to Plattekill, take the New York Thruway north to exit 20 for Kingston. Take Route 28 west for about forty minutes to Arkville. Turn right at Crosby's Farm Equipment onto a cutoff road. Turn right in a mile at the T intersection onto Route 30 north. Follow signs for Plattekill off of Route 30 to the base lodge.

Killington Ski Area, Rutland, Vermont

Killington is located right in the center of Vermont and is a Goliath in terms of eastern ski areas. Killington encompasses six mountain peaks, and has more than 900 acres of skiing on 75 miles of trails with the greatest vertical rise (3150 feet) of any ski resort east of the Rockies. During the summer the Killington Peak chairlift is open to mountain biking and provides 1700 vertical feet of rise. There is a multitude of trails from wide-open fire roads to dense and twisty singletrack on over fifty miles of trails. Trail access for the 1996 season was $8.00 a day. Trail access with one lift ride was $18.00, and unlimited lift use was $25.00 a day. For more information call (802) 422-3261.

DIRECTIONS: From New Jersey the most scenic and direct way to get to Killington is to take the New York Thruway (Interstate 87) north to exit 24. Take 87 north from Albany to exit 20 for Glens Falls. Take 149 east to Route 4. Follow Route 4 through Rutland and up to the Killington Access Road. Follow to the end to the Killington Base Lodge parking lot.

The author at rest

ABOUT THE AUTHOR

Author Joshua Pierce went over the handlebars on June 29, 1981 after "messing around" on his bike and split open his chin to the tune of six stitches and a handsome scar. He's been hooked ever since.

He graduated from Rutgers University in New Jersey in 1993. Since then he has used his degrees in English and History to teach skiing in Colorado and Wyoming, learn the inner workings of retail bicycle stores, become better acquainted with all the great classics (microbrew classics, that is) and write this book.